Patty Kogutek is a spiritual dynamo! She may have had "A Change of Habit" but when it comes to life, never a change of heart. She is all about friendship, family and faith, and writes of all three with verve.

—Adriana Trigiani, Bestselling author of "Big Stone Gap"

★★★

Guilt. Truly the root of all evil! I don't know a single soul who hasn't or doesn't suffer from at least one of the infinite forms guilt takes.

"A Change of Habit" is both entertaining and bittersweet as Patty relays her story and reveals the heavy burden of guilt that plagued her throughout her experience of becoming a nun. She shares her journey from pain and loneliness to freedom and eventual fulfillment with honesty, frankness and humor. Many times I laughed and many times my heart ached for her as I read how, for years, the power of guilt kept her stuck in a place (mentally, emotionally and physically) she yearned to break free of.

Patty's story of setting herself free from what she ultimately realized was a self-imposed prison of guilt is an uplifting read and a fantastic lesson for us all about trusting our own intuition and forging our relationship with God on our own terms, rather than those that are dictated to us."

—Loree Bischoff, Holistic Life Coach and author of "Common Sense Happiness"

★★★

"A Change of Habit" is moving and soul-searching…

—Constance Holcomb, Retired Publishing Executive

A Change of Habit's Honors & Awards

– 2012 THE GREAT NORTHWEST BOOK FESTIVAL
Honorable Mention in Biography/Autobiography Category

– 2012 GREAT SOUTHWEST BOOK FESTIVAL
Runner Up in Spiritual Category

– 2012 SAN FRANCISCO BOOK FESTIVAL
Panelist "The Art of Marketing and Promotion"

– 2012 GREAT SOUTHEAST BOOK FESTIVAL
Runner Up in Spiritual Category

– 2012 SOUTHERN CALIFORNIA BOOK FESTIVAL
First Place in Spiritual Category

– 2012 LOS ANGELES BOOK FESTIVAL
First Place in Spiritual Category

– 2013 NATIONAL INDIE EXCELLENCE AWARDS
Finalist in Memoir Category

– THE HAY HOUSE NEWSLETTER
"Rising Star" Featured Author

– THE BALBOA NEWSLETTER
Featured Author

– 2012 LONDON BOOK FESTIVAL
Runner-Up in Spiritual Category

– 2012 NEW ENGLAND BOOK FESTIVAL
Runner-Up in Spiritual Category

– 2012 NEW ENGLAND BOOK FESTIVAL
Panelist "Write What You Know"

– 2012 PARIS BOOK FESTIVAL
First Place in Spiritual Category

– ARIZONA AUTHOR'S 2012 LITERARY CONTEST
First Place in Published Nonfiction Category

– 2013 INTERNATIONAL BOOK AWARDS
Finalist in Spirituality General Category

– 2013 NEW YORK BOOK FESTIVAL
Honorable Mention

– 2013 GREAT MIDWEST BOOK FESTIVAL
Honorable Mention

A CHANGE OF HABIT

A Spiritual Journey From Sister
Mary Kateri To Sister Mary Vodka

— Revised Edition —

PATTY PTAK KOGUTEK, ED.D.

Books may be ordered through booksellers or by contacting:

Patty Kogutek
www.pattykogutek.com
1-(406) 885-2225

Printed in the United States of America

ISBN 978-0-9968681-1-2

To my parents who were there for me on every
step of my journey.
In thanksgiving and appreciation for their untiring
love and support.

Contents

Preface

Between the years of 1965-2005 the Catholic Church lost sixty-two percent of its nuns.* I am one of those. But despite my struggles with the Church, I never left God.

A Change of Habit begins as the story of my seven years as a Roman Catholic nun. Those powerful formative years shaped my search for God and happiness. But the behaviors I learned in the convent walked out of the nunnery with me.

Even after leaving the convent, I could not escape being the nun. Those three letters, N-U-N, have defined my life, coloring it with hues of black and white. When I divorced my first earthly husband, I remember exclaiming, "Free at last!" But with surprise, I recalled also muttering those same words twelve years earlier when I left the convent. The patterns ingrained in the convent required years to unravel, to the point where I still wrestle with some today.

While I did leave the convent, I never left God. I failed to find God in the rites, rituals, and rules of the Church. But then I asked, "Is He okay, and am I okay with my spiritual search following a path other than the one led by the church hierarchy?" My answer came in happiness.

Six years ago, a spiritual counselor suggested that I write a book to share my story, one she deemed could portray struggles that would be helpful to others. I resisted her suggestion since I had no inclination to share my "nun secret" so publicly. I wanted to hide the fact that I was a nun. In the mid-1960s, President Kennedy challenged youth of my generation to serve. Entering the Peace Corps to go to a foreign country seemed more exotic than entering a convent adjacent to my high school. Being a nun wasn't cool. But as a "guilt sponge," I tucked the urging in the back of my mind.

Two years sped by, and I spent a winter in Arizona. While meeting new people, the "nun secret" emerged. People were, as always, fascinated by the nun years of my life wanting to know why I entered such a strange lifestyle, what was it like in the convent, and why I left religious life. Later, I met with a life coach who challenged me to write fifteen minutes a day beginning chronologically from birth. I took up that challenge, which evolved into scenes of this book.

Writing proved difficult. It required scouring my soul for painful things that I had so neatly stuffed away. On many days, I had to abandon writing because of tears or getting emotionally exhausted. But in return, the book turned out to be a cathartic journal.

I wrote my story to help others find happiness through adversity by breaking through the bondage of guilt. We each have our own journeys, but that doesn't mean that we have to go it alone. My words are meant to be of support and consolation to my fellow spiritual sojourners–those struggling to do the "right thing."

A Change of Habit, with my departure from the convent and testing conventional Catholicism, is in no way meant to take swipes at the Catholic Church, the convent, or nuns that taught me in school. Every Catholic school, every religious convent, and every Catholic family embraced values of commitment, obedience, and discipline with high expectations. Placed in the time prior to Vatican II, the religious practices depicted within my story were normal. The religious trifecta— the Church, my strict Catholic home, and the religious sisters—made me who I am today.

Convents have changed in the past fifty years. The accepted religious practices of my experience seem archaic and severe by today's standards. Sharing my journey is by no means intended to be offensive to anyone. I am thankful for the dedicated nuns who have devoted their lives to the service of others. If you find yourself bristling, please read on trusting that everything works out for the best, a spiritual renaissance.

This is my story as I lived it. It's a story of love, searching, change, responsibility, and hope. The choices I made wove the fabric of my life...for worse and for better. I write as a call to action, moving others to honestly and continuously reflect on their own situations and bravely act to promote and protect their own power and happiness. No matter where you are on your life's path or what religion you may practice, enjoy my journey of discovery as I share the "secrets" that I've collected along my way.

—Patty Ptak Kogutek

---

* "State of the U.S. Catholic Church at the Beginning of 2006," by Father John McCloskey.

Chapter 1

Packing Black

Choosing my own clothing that day was the last decision I made for myself. I selected my blue and gray plaid skirt with a matching blue cashmere-like sweater for Sunday church.

After arriving home from Mass that morning in September, I had just enough time to fold the last of my new clothing into the black suitcase. We had purchased all the items on the nun checklist—even down to the industrial black shoes that I'd picked out with seven of my girlfriends on a shopping trip. The convent had sent a list of items to bring with me the day of entry—kind of like getting ready to go to summer convent camp.

While my high school girlfriends crammed trunks with new colorful fashions for their first year of college, I packed the nun list of drab, dire, black skirts and blouses for practical use, not adornment. I left my pink lacy bras and panties in the drawer, bringing instead the big white cotton granny-type underpants. Those and a few long-sleeved white blouses provided the only deviation from prescribed black. I pushed the black out of my head, assuring myself that the happiness the nuns exuded would make up for the dour lack of color.

No sooner had I latched the suitcase lid, than my sister Penny waltzed into my bedroom. With hangers of skirts draping over her arms, she aimed to claim my closet.

"Can't you wait just one more day? Get out of my room!" I shouted at the invader.

"Make me," she taunted, poking her boney finger in my arm to up the confrontation. "It's going to be my room soon, so you'd better get used to it."

"Out!" I hissed, grabbing her arm and leading her to the door. She kicked me. So I pounced on her, taking us both to the floor.

"What's going on here, you two? Break this up right now," Mom intervened. Despite the nun clothes folded in my suitcase, I displayed far from nun-like behavior at that moment. But Mom sided with me, most likely due to my imminent departure.

"I think it's time to go, Pat," Dad called up the stairs, a forced cheeriness in his voice. Glancing around my bedroom for the last time, I took visual snapshots of all the record albums, pictures of girlfriends on my bulletin board, my stuffed dog, and my closet jammed with a rainbow of color. With an inkling of regret, but knowing that the road to holiness was lined with sacrifice, I took my first step down the path to religious fulfillment by parting with my favorite things. I picked up the suitcase to face my final farewells to the family.

I tiptoed into Robbie's bedroom and kissed my three-month-old brother. I remembered that day when Dad came home from the hospital looking exhausted but delighted to say we finally had a baby brother. He and Mom had been raising kids for eighteen years, and they were just starting over with diapers again.

One by one, the family assembled in the living room. I hugged each one of my three sisters, even Penny. I muttered quick good-byes for fear of breaking into sobs. Nothing had equipped me to face the finality of leaving my family. My friends all marched off to college, knowing they could call or come home at the first holiday, but my future held no such promises. While the convent sat only twenty-five minutes across town, it might as well have been on a different planet.

Fulfilling my role as the responsible firstborn, I handed the reins of oldest sister to Penny: "Now you will be number one. Take good care of them." That did it. Both of us burst into tears knowing that our family unit would be forever changed.

To avoid prolonging the pain, I ran to join Mom and Dad in the car and huddled in the back seat. I buried my teary face in my arm propped on the window.

On the drive to the convent, no one spoke. Dad stared at the road ahead. Mom rubbed her hands together, fixing blank eyes out the passenger window. Over the past several weeks, my parents had grown quieter, oftentimes staring at me for no apparent reason. Dad's eyes held a tired, sad cast, while Mom seemed to run on super octane to avoid facing the fact that I had chosen to pursue a life married to God.

"Patty," Dad broke the stillness, looking in the rearview mirror at me. "You know how proud we are of you for doing this. If there's anything you need in there, just let us know." Words were at a premium. Dad, usually the more emotional one of my parents, kept himself in check. No one wanted to open the floodgates.

"I think I have everything I need," I managed to eke out without gushing into more tears. Mom, businesslike, nodded her head in agreement.

We turned into the big circular driveway of my all girls' Catholic high school and the convent. Arching elms graced the roadway, which swung first past the two-story high school. I peered at the building as if its familiarity could ease my tenseness. Voices from my high school days seemed to drift from its brick walls.

"Next," thundered Sister Mary Cleopha in my tenth grade algebra class. Up and down the aisles in round robin fashion, we sought out "X" as the unknown in algebra equations.

As my turn approached, my stomach knotted into a familiar tangle. I flipped ahead through my steno notebook searching to find the exact problem I'd have to answer. "Oh shit, not this one," I whimpered when I saw it.

My tongue swelled in my parched mouth as I began my oral performance. With shoulders hunched over my tablet, my eyes fastened onto the problem at hand, I read the formula: "3x plus 8 (9 subtract y)." I paused, stumbling at my stupid error. "3x plus," I began again in a weak, quavering voice, knowing that starting over was strictly forbidden.

"Dora Dumbhead," Sister Cleopha screamed, slamming the desk with her red plastic ruler, almost shattering it. "Do you want to be boiled in oil, hung by your thumbs, or shot at dawn?" I cowered in my desk. The other students tried to stifle grins, while their eyes empathized with me. No one escaped the wrath of Sister Mary Cleopha; she had targeted each of the girls in my class at one time or another. Her tirades appeared with such frequency that they became her trademark.

I slunk lower in my seat, trying to make myself invisible as my head hung. Sister Cleopha set her teeth and locked her jaw. "Well, Dora, what's it going to be?" she demanded, pushing me to answer her question as she pounded her palm on the desk.

Silence hung over the class like a stifling humid night. Tears welled into my eyes, as I sniffled in hopes of randomly choosing the correct answer.

"Boiled in oil?" I whispered. I could almost feel the piercing glare of Sister Cleopha and picture orange flames shooting from her nostrils.

"Skip!" she pronounced and dropped me from her mathematical clutches to move to her next victim.

After school, I had run home to beg my father to let me drop out of Cleopha's class. Wincing on the couch, I faced Dad who sat upright looking straight at me.

"Patty, our family has a strong faith. We believe that God will take care of us, in good times and dark days. God leads us through his representatives—the Pope, bishops, priests, and nuns." He spoke to me as if speaking to someone in elementary school, not in high school.

"God wants me to suffer in Cleopha's class?" I glared at him.

Dad's eyes softened with understanding, but he resumed his litany with steadfast determination to make me understand. "Our Pope is infallible in leading the church. The priests and nuns have a special calling to act as His ministers. We must obey them as we would obey God Himself. God speaks to us though his priests and nuns. They act in His behalf as His spokesmen."

I soaked up his words.

"I know this is difficult for you to accept right now," Dad attempted to comfort me. "Just accept God's way as shown through Sister Mary Cleopha. We owe obedience to the church and its representatives, even though it may be a challenge and we don't understand it sometimes. It's our responsibility as Catholics to follow the will of the church."

""You are the oldest child," Dad continued, launching into a familiar tune—one that ran as a theme throughout my eighteen years. "You have to be responsible for your siblings. They look up to you to lead the way by always doing the right thing."

"I know. I get it," I mumbled through tears. "I'll stick with the class." I wiped my salty face with the back of my hand. I would submit to the church and its representative nuns and priests. I would do what was necessary to please them all, for that meant pleasing God.

As I stared at my high school building that served as the educational preparation for 400 of us girls, my eyes watered. Unlike my girlfriends with their carefree spirits, obedience ran in my mind like a tape recorder on continuous play. When my dad swung into his obedience lecture, I always knew the words before they spilled from his mouth: "We have high expectations for you, and we know that you will make us proud." The same words resonated through the Catholic homes of my friends, too, but the message seemed to hit me harder.

The words—laden with the weight of responsibility as the firstborn—worked as they always did on me. They whittled me into an obedient daughter, ready to do the bidding of my father, the church, and God, pleasing everyone and making them proud.

As we drove under the elms, I remembered how they looked last winter, festooned with white toilet paper. Sister Constantine, our principal, had railed at us over the intercom demanding that the guilty party come forward to confess. Scowling to reinforce high behavior standards, she meted out punishments for minor infractions in demerits that culminated in detention and other punishments. Gossip said that one girl who committed a major infraction had to clean the lavatory with a toothbrush. I hadn't been responsible for the Charmin decorating the elm trees, but the Sister's command carried religious power: "We know who did this, and we want to you to come forward." The thought of her words still shot a bolt of guilt through me as if I had.

I absorbed the guilt thrown out by the nuns. Their mantras rang in my head at every turn: "Don't be selfish. Always think of others' needs before your own. You can always be better. Aim for being holy. Strive for perfection." I wanted to please them, so I soaked up the guilt without question. They expected high standards that left no room for failure.

As the driveway curved further, the school slipped from my vision, and the convent rose giant by comparison. My stomach dropped to my feet. The convent stood, an immense, intimidating, towering mass of red brick with small uniform windows. No curtains, no color.

I had driven up this circle many times to school, but never given much thought to the massive convent. Most of it had been off-limits to students. We were only permitted to go in the convent chapel and downstairs auditorium via the closest entry from the high school.

The goings-on inside the convent held mystery. The black-draped nuns floated into school or the chapel in their habits, appearing legless, their ethereal gait hinting at serene joy. They gave nary an inkling to what they did inside. We never saw them go on a walk or eat.

Other than the chapel and auditorium, I had never before pierced the sacred veil of the convent. The double glass doors, while appearing airy and friendly on the outside, bore a reflective privacy coating blocking inquisitive eyes. Contrary to the familiar warmth of the chapel interior, the cold brick convent exterior looked more like a factory. A wave of panic rose as I realized that this formidable building would be my new home.

"Is it too late to change my mind?" the words flickered through me, threatening to unravel my composure. I wanted to ask to my parents if I could change my plans, but I kept silent. I had been called by God to be a nun. I couldn't say no to God or His special calling.

As Dad pulled up to the imposing convent entrance, I knew I couldn't reverse my decision. I couldn't disappoint my family, the nuns, or God. Dad retrieved my suitcase from the trunk. The three of us looked at the cement steps, hesitating for a brief moment, each of us knowing what walking up the steps meant. We climbed up the steps without a word, Mom and Dad flanking me to the double glass threshold. Setting the lone bag on the cement, Dad rang the bell. Its shrill sound reverberated down the empty convent corridors.

An unfamiliar nun opened the door. Anticipating the recognizable features of one of my high school teachers, I stepped back, jolted by the stranger.

"Come in," the Sister offered a polite invitation. "We were expecting you. Come this way."

We walked through the doors. On the inside, a steel panel barred the door's middle to prevent anyone escaping from the inside. Bile rose in my stomach, which I squelched by looking ahead into the hall.

The nun led us down an unlit hallway into the stark receiving parlor. She deposited us in the parlor to wait. As she departed, she announced in a voice aloof with control that the Novice Mistress would soon join us.

Mom and Dad sat on one of the two couches. I took a seat on one of the adjacent four Queen Anne chairs. We looked around in spellbound silence. Wavering on the edge of sobs, I felt safety in the silence, unable to count on my voice to speak. To divert my attention, I inventoried the room.

The wooden floors shone like they had been spit-shined by a Navy crew. Two small glass-paned windows filtered light through lacy curtains, illuminating a well-worn oriental rug on the floor. The wall held paintings— one of the Annunciation of Mary and another showing her receiving the dead body of her Son after his death on the cross.

"Pretty somber," I thought, wondering what the rest of the convent looked like. I hoped the nunnery proved a little homier than this bleak room that could pass for an alcove in a museum, so silent, so eerie. My stomach churned at the contrast with our warm family home, where the walls cluttered with photos of our childhood and relatives.

Looking at my dad's resignation, I felt submission fall over me, too. "God picked me," I reminded myself. My mind flashed back almost two years earlier. Father Damian had framed my decision to be a nun during a three-day junior retreat in the chapel.

As Father Damian stood before us, robed in a long brown Franciscan tunic cinched by a simple white rope, he stared down at rows of identically clad girls. We appeared as little soldiers waiting for orders, clothed in the mandated, nondescript, blue school uniforms serge skirts with matching plain sleeveless jackets, crisp clean white shirts with the approved collars, and blue or white hair ribbons. Jewelry was a no-no, except for religious medals.

He'd already exhorted us with a long list of religious dos and don'ts. We were told to pray, obey God and His church, and sacrifice ourselves. He'd emphasized shunning mortal and venial sin, lecturing us on the evils of steady dating, which were punishable by expulsion from school. We inwardly rolled our eyes. On the third day, he readied to conclude the retreat.

"My dear students in Christ," he began his standard sermon that dripped with routine. "Today we are going to explore the special calling from God, a vocation." I groaned inside at the annual lecture to think about being nuns. "A vocation is a very special gift from God Himself only bestowed upon a chosen few. These specially selected children of God are called to serve Him as a priest or nun," Father Damian prattled on.

He swept his eyes across the mass of girls as he began to itemize what was expected: "First of all, a girl needs to have a committed love to God Almighty."

I guffawed inside. No one would admit to not loving God. That would be stupid.

Father Damian's second requirement—a deep devotion to the church—seemed equally as obvious. After all, our parents made sacrifices to send us to Catholic school where we learned about the church. We all went to Mass, where I loved hearing the lofty music and smelling the heady mix of flowers and incense—a heavenly perfume— that catapulted me into a prayerful silence with God.

The Father forged on narrowing the field, "Thirdly, this young woman needs to have a reverence for her spiritual growth." Several of my friends displayed little concern for spiritual growth, but as a three-year member of a special club for those girls wanting to grow spiritually, I had been tallying my daily religious actions on a dittoed checklist. I recited the rosary, examined my conscience, and devoted fifteen minutes to spiritual reading.

"The fourth quality is a dedication to the service of the church," he pronounced. This, too, seemed like a given as every girl I knew seemed dedicated to serving the church. Even in grade school, we tossed our coins into little milk cartons on our desks to send missionaries to spread the Catholic message to pagan babies around the world. I served the church by singing in the choir and holding bake sales. I glanced around the room to see how the rest of the girls absorbed his words and sat up straight, proud of my service.

But then, ticking off the four traits that Father Damian mentioned, I gripped my rosary. If I matched up with the fifth quality, I would qualify to be a nun. Sometimes as a little girl, I would play "nun," designing chapels out of living room furniture and throwing a towel over my head for a veil, but I never seriously considered joining their ranks. Nuns had taught me since kindergarten. They were mysterious, hiding behind black concealing habits. I'd never even seen one take a bite of food.

Wriggling in discomfort, I shuffled my posture on the bench, tenseness creeping into my shoulders. I wasn't sure I wanted to be a nun. But I already matched four of the qualities that the Father identified. Clutching my rosary, I hung on the Father's words.

Drawing his body upright and raking his eyes once more across the room, Father Damian squared himself in front of us, his stance indicating he broached the most important quality. "This special girl," he began in a powerful tone intended to drive our duty home, "would have a priest or a nun encourage her to enter the convent and religious life." I released air through my pursed lips and dropped my earlobe-high shoulders. No nun had encouraged me to enter the convent. I hoped no one else noticed my relief, but I was glad I didn't meet the standard to be a nun with the divine summons.

Five months later, Father Talbot, our parish priest, joined our family for a Sunday dinner to ask my parents for money to expand the parish schools. Of course, my dad, a good Catholic servant of the church, agreed to contribute to the special fund. Then, Father Talbot probed Penny and me about our future plans. I babbled about my school newspaper column, "Patty's Peephole," and maybe studying journalism at the University of Nebraska.

When I'd run out of things to say, Father Talbot squared his eyes at me, setting down his fork just as he had with my father about the money. He spoke in a studied voice, "Have you ever thought about becoming a nun? You know, Patty, with your many talents and personality, you would make a wonderful nun. Give the idea some thought and prayer." Bells clanged inwardly, shaping an abrupt turn in my life without my parents or family aware of the import of Father Talbot's words.

That night in my room, I shuddered at the thought of being a nun, but my stomach heaved more at the punishment for turning down God's special invitation to be a nun. I could not suffer a life of retribution for turning Him down. I could no more say "no" to Father Talbot, the emissary of God, than my dad could say "no" to giving money to the parish. I knew I now matched all five of Father Damian's requirements to be a nun. Father Talbot's words carried the weight of God, compelling me to obey as if they were a command.

"God, are you there? It's me, Patty," I prayed. "Where are you, and what do you want? I'm listening." I had always relied on The Lord's Prayer, the Our Father. But now, the words rang through my heart: "Thy will be done on earth as it is in heaven."

I waited for God's voice to tell me to be a nun, so I could then respond with "yes." But I knew His request had already been spoken through Father Talbot. God had chosen me to be a nun. The calling required no decision on my part. I would obey.

As I sat in the receiving parlor with my parents waiting for the Novice Mistress, I knew with certainty that God had called me to be a nun. His message came through the priests, loud and clear. My duty was to follow that calling. I resigned myself to my future.

Silence weighed heavy in the room. I wanted to say so much to my parents, but didn't know where to start. Dad's pained eyes across the room spoke volumes. No need for words.

Soon, the Novice Mistress floated in with a forced smile on her face. The strained situation hardly deserved the gaiety she showed. In automatic reaction, my stomach clenched with fear.

As we all rose to attention, she made no move to relax us. She stood as stoic as a statue to introduce herself as Mother Monica and then embraced both of my parents' hands. Everything about her moved like a robot in precise sharp staccato motion.

"My job is to prepare these young candidates for the taking of their vows at the end of the second year," she announced with stern eyes. Then she added the qualifier, "Providing they meet our standards." The hairs on the back of my neck bristled. "I do have the five qualities that Father Damian listed to make a good nun," I proudly shot back in my mind.

"Your job," she instructed Mom and Dad, "is to obey the rules I set down and pray that your daughter will have the strength she will need to endure her special calling." Both of my parents nodded in silent agreement, understanding the church, and therefore God, made the rules.

"We have very strict guidelines for these first two years," Mother Monica continued, throwing her shoulders back in command as if lecturing school children about playground rules. "This makes it easier for the candidates to make the break from their families and the world they once knew."

"For the first month, there will be little communication with you," she directed her comments to my parents. "Trust me. If there is a need, I will contact you." I fought back the tears welling up and wondered whether my parents knew about the rules.

"Then, there will be weekly supervised letter correspondence," Mother Monica continued with the rules of contact. "Patty will have no access to a phone, so writing will be your only method of communication. Following the first month, if I feel the appropriate separation has occurred, you may come to visit your daughter for one hour."

Whoa. The list of rules blindsided me. I never imagined that the nuns would sever ties between my family and me, but none of us spoke up to object. Mom, Dad, and I absorbed the new rules of our relationship as dictated by the convent. We shook our heads in agreement, knowing that the church had the authority to do what was best for us.

Mother Monica's list of rules concluded my "welcome" into the convent. As she reached out for Dad's hand, she shook it with confidence, boring into his wet eyes. "Thank you for giving us your daughter," she enunciated. Those words hung in mid air. Dad's resounding silence pierced my heart.

After a tearful, rushed good-bye, she ushered my parents out of the parlor. With crestfallen shoulders, Dad reached for Mom's hand, leading her to the door. "Wait for me. I want to go, too," I yelled in my head. But instead, I watched them walk away. I wondered if my parents felt the loss as keenly as I did.

Mother Monica wasted no time with chatter. Floating, she led me out of the parlor. I dragged behind, carrying my suitcase that weighed more with each step. She marched me through golden-varnished doubled French doors that should have felt quaint and cozy, but in the convent setting seemed austere. They clanged and latched shut. Locking out the world and locking me in.

Chapter 2

Molding in Religious Boot Camp

"**G**od, it's me, Patty. I'm really in here. Don't leave me now," I whispered, begging for comfort as Mother Monica led me through the convent to the novitiate. Looking for an extended hand to clasp, I found none—just solemn walls and the Mother's black back. Her rigid posture emitted a grim "hands off."

Connected to the modern industrial convent building by a hallway, the three-story brick novitiate could pass for a bed and breakfast, appearing so tiny in contrast. On wobbling legs, I followed Mother Monica through the honey-colored oak doors into the novitiate. The heavy doors thumped closed, echoing down the empty corridors. I noticed a key in the lock, wondering if that key kept people out or nuns shut in.

Trudging through the novitiate behind Mother Monica, I took in the spartan building. The novitiate would be my home for the next two years. It housed the first year candidates-in-training called postulants and the second year novices, who wore the full habits of nuns with white veils. Following the two-year novitiate program, novices then took temporary vows to be junior professed nuns. They received black veils and moved to the adjacent main convent building.

On the novitiate's main floor, we entered an enormous community room that served as a gathering place. On its walls, reproductions of famous religious artwork conveyed severity rather than friendliness. Twenty single desks formed a classroom on one side of the community room while chairs and sofas created a recreation side. I spotted an office that must be Mother Monica's off to the side, wondering if that, too, would be a place to avoid at all costs like the office of our high school principal Sister Constantine.

Contrary to home, where a stereo, radio, television, newspapers, and magazines filled the living room, the novitiate's community room seemed bare. I wondered how we would keep up on what was happening in the world. My high school government teacher, the only male in the school, drilled into us that good adults stayed up-to-date on the news. We followed social and political issues of the early Sixties—the introduction of birth control pills, U.S. combat troops shipping off to the Vietnam War, and the civil rights movement sweeping through cities with sit-ins, demonstrations, and marches. But the quiet, clean community room seemed a world apart from these forces. Not one magazine or newspaper hinted at the world beyond the novitiate doors.

Mother Monica led me to the other eight incoming postulants sitting on the chairs and sofas. No one spoke. Eight pairs of eyes stared at me.

Searching the room for a friendly face, I zeroed in on Judy one of my friends at school who joined me on the nun shoe-shopping trip. With my back toward Mother Monica, I aimed to claim the empty spot next to Judy and jutted my lower jaw forward with a mute "Eek." I expected a smile of recognition, but Judy stared right through me with a blank face. Fear crouching in my stomach clawed up toward my throat.

"This is Patty," Mother Monica introduced me to the eight other girls. Muffled "hellos" welcomed me, accompanied by flat expressions rank with dread.

Mother Monica sat stern-faced at the head of the circle of us nine girls, much like a proud peacock, but lacking bright colors. Only her ashen white face and pasty hands stuck out from under the black habit. The headpiece atop her petite frame seemed to squeeze her round apple doll features. Instead of softening her appearance, her blue eyes smoldered steely cold, unrelenting. Instincts warned me to avoid eye contact.

She sat rigid. With her knees pinched together, her feet flat on the floor, and her marble white hands folded neatly in her lap, she modeled how a good nun sat. I picked up the hint and uncrossed my legs, intersecting my ankles instead.

Mother Monica took charge. Rather than letting us speak for ourselves, she introduced us, disseminating the three pieces of information that she deemed important: our names, what schools we had attended, and where we lived. I noticed that the four big high schools staffed by the order each sent two postulants. My thoughts flashed back to a friend's assertion that the nuns groomed certain girls to enter the convent. She might have been correct with each school having a quota of two candidates. The ninth girl wanted to follow in her aunt's footsteps in the order.

"Welcome to your new family," Mother Monica greeted us, composing her unadorned colorless lips with a cool plastic smile. "I'm pleased to have you all as our new postulant class. You have all come here with the intention of serving God. I am here to you're your with your spiritual journey."

I stole a glance around at my new "family." Debbie, leaning forward as if not to miss a word, looked like she had been counting the days until her arrival. Her broad smile and almost giddy demeanor could win a "Miss Congeniality" award in any beauty pageant. "Too excited," I thought. The others wore grim expressions, nothing close to the convival gaiety of my high school friends.

"During this year of probation called postulantancy," continued Mother Monica, "I will be looking at you to assess your fitness for the religious life as a nun." She expanded on what our two years in the novitiate would be like—including the regular college classes we'd be taking on the premises, all in preparation to be sent out on a teaching mission one day. Her serious eyes bored holes into us as she painted a verbal picture of the year to come. Attending college classes sounded normal for an eighteen-year-old. It was the only hint of normalcy in her portrait of our convent lives.

"But the main focus for this year is your spiritual growth," she pinpointed, eyeing each one of us as if we were lumps of clay fit for her molding. "My duty is to guide you in determining if you are a worthy candidate for religious life. Those who successfully complete this first year as a postulant will continue here in the novitiate as a novice. This cloistered time concentrates on the vows of poverty, chastity, and obedience that nuns profess before getting the black veil."

Poverty, chastity, and obedience. I steeled myself to concentrate on those virtues. After all, I'd been chosen by God through his priests to be a nun. Poverty, chastity, and obedience were the terms of the deal, and I would show Mother Monica just how good of a nun I could be, especially since God singled me out with this religious vocation.

"This is a special time for you to give yourself to God," Mother Monica enunciated every word. "In order to facilitate your communication with the Divine, we will concentrate on the spiritual world, leaving the materialistic world behind. You will not see a television, hear a radio, read a newspaper, or talk on the telephone. You will be making a break with the world you know in order to find your life in the spiritual realm."

I felt as if an axe dropped, chopping the world off from me, cutting away what had been part of my daily routine. "Newspapers and television are one thing, but not talk on the telephone? But what about my family? What about my friends?" I panicked, but then remembered the rules she'd spelled out with my parents. I wanted to ask "what is wrong with the outside world that God created?" But Mother Monica's stern eyes forbade questions, and the stifling air in the room reinforced that she snubbed out challenges.

I snatched a glance around the room to see how the others reacted. With arched eyebrows, Liz held a fixed startled expression akin to just seeing a ghost. Her coupled hands trembled, and her breathing came in short gasps for air. But Mother Monica ignored Liz and shifted the grave mood.

Inviting us to follow her, Mother Monica rose to march downstairs for tea in the dining room. She instructed us to call it the refectory.

Like ducklings, waddling after the mother duck, we obedient postulants followed Mother Monica down the flight of cement steps into the chilly dim refectory with its chalky tan and dark brown tiled floor. Two long tables stretched down the sides of the room. Places set only on one side of each table allowed each sister to face the middle of the room. At the head of the two tables, a smaller table held a place setting for one person, Mother Monica. From this vantage point, at the center of the "U" formation, the Novice Mistress could appraise all of us, as we ate. The formal arrangement jarred me. It drew such a contrast to my home with its round table topped by a spinning Lazy Susan.

We found our assigned seats identified by name cards. The seating arrangement split up girls from the same high school while the novices sat at the opposite table.

Standing at the head of the room, Mother Monica began a second lecture: "Since our religious Mother order, the Sisters of Mary, originated in England, it is our custom to have tea every day at 3:30." Two of the white-veiled novices rolled in an industrial silver metal cart with coffee, tea, and platters of cake.

We sat silent, waiting for the next instruction as Mother Monica clearly had more to say. Next to me, Eileen jiggled her knee up and down. Taking a cue from the more experienced novices, who hid their hands under their robes, I locked my jittery hands together in my lap to listen to the Novice Mistress's words.

Mother Monica launched into a lesson about the rule of silence for the novitiate. The rule forbade speaking, restricting conversation to certain places, at prescribed times, about designated subjects. A little ringing hand bell would signal when talking was permitted. No one dared to ask a question of clarification.

Mother Monica tinkled the bell. Quiet, polite conversation started. Hands passed the platters of cake down the rows for each sister to take a slice. Taciturn, Eileen chewed her cake, perhaps feeling shy about initiating conversation. As I picked up my fork for strength, I threw out the first words.

"If I remember right, you're from Detroit?"

"Yes. My older sister is a novice here. She is the one over there." Beaming at the chance to share something personal, she pointed to a smiling novice sitting at the opposite table. "Her name is Sister Mary Faith. I want to be a nun, too."

We chatted about our families and schools. While Eileen enjoyed her cake, my knotted up stomach left me with no appetite. When the cake platter came around for seconds, I passed it on to Eileen, who took another slice. Mother Monica took note.

She jingled the tiny bell again, indicating that conversation should cease. In her unrelenting voice, she resumed instruction: "We eat to live, not live to eat." Her eyes bored into Eileen. Silence hung heavy. My heart ached for Eileen, who seemed to be singled out for humiliation and yet wanted to be a good nun. The lesson from Mother Monica put a damper on the rest of teatime.

Abruptly, Mother Monica stood up, signaling the end of tea. "The novices will now take you to the third floor to show you where you will be sleeping," she commanded, like organizing a brigade. "Your bags are there for you to unpack. Dress in your postulant attire and meet me back in the community room when you have completed your induction."

Following the white-veiled novices, wondering if they too felt fear on their first day in the novitiate, we marched from the basement level of the refectory to climb two flights of steps, past the community room, up to the third floor. The top floor housed the dormitory where the postulants and novices slept, the community bathroom, a small classroom, and Mother Monica's private bedroom.

With sunlight streaming through the windows, the enormous dorm lit up brightly with the most light of any room in the novitiate. At first glance, the dorm appeared similar to a hospital infirmary with a shiny, waxed tile floor and twenty beds made up with crisp white cotton bedspreads. Metal railings supported white starched, creased curtains intended to provide privacy between beds. Next to each bed stood a small wooden chair and a small waist-high chest containing three drawers. The dorm appeared as if it could pass antiseptic hospital standards.

"This is how nuns live," I thought to myself remembering all the speculation among my friends in school. As I surveyed the room, my stomach twisted at the thought of my spacious bedroom at home: my large blue bed loaded with stuffed animals, my favorite gray stuffed dog, my color-coordinated furniture, and my stereo. The memory clashed against the tiny cheerless white curtained cubicles. I wondered how different Mother Monica's room was.

Sister Mary Faith, Eileen's sister, led me over to a bed by a window. "This is your cell, Patty," she welcomed me with the first warm smile I'd seen. But the term "cell" sounded so cold and sterile. My stomach churned in reaction.

"This will be for your personal washing," Sister Mary Faith continued, opening the top drawer to take out a large basin and a water jug. "You will need to go into the common restroom area to retrieve your water to wash and brush your teeth." My jaw gaped. I had never considered that nuns didn't have running water and sinks for washing. "We live in community as the first Christians did," the Sister justified the routine.

Glancing over her shoulder to check the whereabouts of her younger sister, Sister Mary Faith continued my indoctrination into the fine art of communal living as she led me to the community restroom. Two partitioned bathtub areas, three commode stalls, and two sinks comprised the shared bathroom for seventeen women. "You may use the tubs for bathing either in the morning when you awaken or at night before you go to sleep," the Sister doled out more bathroom rules, not waiting for my questions or reaction.

Sister Mary Faith then led me to a big oversized dresser outside Mother Monica's bedroom. A large notepad and pen rested on the dresser. "This pad is for you to request items that you might need, such as toothpaste, soap, or shampoo," the Sister explained, tossing the words out with a hint of caution in her voice.

I snuck a peek at the message on the notepad: "Dear Mother Monica, May I please have a bar of soap. Thank you, and God Bless You, Sister Mary Claudia."

My eyes must have rounded in surprise at having to ask for soap, as Sister Mary Faith jumped to defend the note. "As I said before, we live in community, so we have no personal possessions. Everything belongs to us all. We refer to all possessions as 'ours.'" My brain roiled trying to grasp the new language and new rules.

Leading me back to my cell, Sister Mary Faith instructed me to unpack and dress in my postulant garb. A slight smile snickered across her face as she uttered her next directions: "Leave all of your street clothes and personal items, such as makeup and lipstick, on this chair. You won't be needing those things ever again."

The emphasis on the word "ever" clanged like another door closing on my past and locking me in to my future. "No need to remember all those makeup tricks I used to peruse in Teen magazine," I thought with sarcasm to give myself a little levity.

As Sister Mary Faith left me, I opened my small suitcase to unpack all my worldly possessions that were now "ours." I stowed "our" toothbrush, "our" hairbrush, and "our" small hand mirror in the top drawer. In contrast to my drawers at home overstuffed with hair and jewelry adornments, my new drawers seemed empty.

Arranging my black hose, white underwear, and white long sleeve blouses in the second drawer, I thought about my high school girlfriends who were moving into their college dorms unpacking their bright sweaters and school pep outfits. The thought of their expansive world of color soured my monochrome black and white. My peers launched into living on their own, away from home, discovering freedom and independence; I was submitting my will to Mother Monica, silence, and the rules of the order. I bit my lower lip, fighting back the tears of doubt.

Like peeling off a part of me—my solitary tie to the world outside—I shed my chosen clothes for the required postulant garb. I caressed my blue skirt and matching soft sweater folding them with fond memories. I donned my white blouse and black skirt, then chided myself for thinking of them as "mine" rather than "ours." Tears threatened to spill, but I countered them with reminding myself that I'd been chosen by God for this life.

Before I had a chance to put on my new black opaque stockings, Debbie walked over to my cell and whispered, "Where are the mirrors? I didn't see any anywhere."

Assuming that talking would be off limits here in the dorm, I whispered, "I don't think that there are any. I bought a small hand mirror like the list suggested. Here, use mine," I offered, hoping she wouldn't notice my red eyes.

"Oh, I must have missed that item," Debbie giggled. "I'll have to write to Mother Monica already to ask her for a mirror. She's going to think that I'm a real loser."

"She won't think that at all," I rushed to reassure her, but guessing that Mother Monica would indeed scoff at her request. No doubt, judging every behavior helped Mother Monica make the decision about our fitness as a potential nun.

I pulled on the long black stockings followed by the cloddy industrial nun shoes and looked at myself. The shapeless black and white postulant's garb made our school uniforms look like haute couture. The nuns at school had always kept a keen eye on our clothing and punished those who spurned the dress code. Glancing down at my black postulant skirt, I remembered my mom ensuring that my school uniform hem reached the floor when I knelt, according to the school rule. The memory linked to Sister Mary Cleopha railing at a friend of mine.

"Look at that uniform skirt. On the floor," Sister Mary Cleopha exacted in a tone befitting a marine drill sergeant. "And wipe that grin off your face." As Paige dropped to her knees on the cold linoleum at Sister Mary Cleopha's feet, she winced under the Sister's ferocious eyes. Kneeling, Paige's skirt hem hung a good three inches above the floor where the length was supposed to reach.

"Off to the office with you," Sister Cleopha snorted in disgust. "And don't return until you are properly clothed."

Red-faced, Paige arose to go to the principal's office to call home. But before she could clear out to safety, Sister Cleopha erupted again like an ever-active volcano, "Give me your demerit card. You'll spend a few hours in detention to remind yourself of the school uniform rule."

Fumbling in her pencil case for the blue demerit card, Paige cringed handing the tattered record card to the Sister. Sister Mary Cleopha scanned the numerous punches, marks for the many lapses in proper behavior. "If you want to continue

attending St. Mary's High School, you might review the
rules," the Sister warned Paige.

With Sister Mary Cleopha's words echoing in my head, I stared down at my black serge skirt that far surpassed the hem of my high school skirt. It hung so limply compared to the stylish stitched down skirt that it replaced. It had no shape. It wasn't "A" line. It wasn't pleated. The black skirt looked like an old curtain sagging from waist to mid-calf.

I fought back tears, wondering if we would have to parade our new attire before a nun review board at the convent like we did in high school. Even our prom dresses had been inspected for modesty to check that the sleeves stretched down to three-quarters length and the neckline dropped no lower than two fingers below the neck bone. We all feared expulsion like Beverly, who held up her dress for approval from the board, but later at the dance, whisked around the floor revealing its shocking backlessness. During our Modesty Crusade Fashion Show the week before prom, the nuns reinforced how we should dress with proper decorum. They chose the theme "How Jackie Kennedy would dress in Mary-like clothes." The fashion rules personified the meek and humble Blessed Virgin Mary, who would never be so brash as to expose her arms or cleavage.

"How far from Jackie Kennedy I look in this bag-like attire," I sighed. "But I had better get used to black." I reminded myself that my new attire served as one of the first steps to make me into what God wanted. It was mine until I took the white veil as a novice next August—providing that Mother Monica approved of me.

Back in the community room, the postulants came together clad in identical black clothes. Not speaking, we sat baffled about what to do. "But these shell-shocked girls next to me are my new sisters," I reminded myself to counter the pangs spinning within me. "They're my new family, and this is my new home." Telling myself that my birth family was part of my past worldly life, I sat up straight ready to learn to be a nun.

"My, how lovely you look in your new postulant attire," Mother Monica greeted us as she floated into the room. Her steely blue eyes seemed to soften at sight of our first steps from banishing individuality in favor of conformity.

"In a few minutes, we will be going to the chapel to chant part of the Divine Office called Vespers. Today, you will just watch, listen, and pray the Psalms with us as we chant the prayers. Very soon, you too will be chanting the Psalms with the rest of us," she spoon-fed us the instruction. We sucked it up like obedient children eager to learn.

But to complete our postulant attire, we needed veils to enter the chapel. The novices helped us bobby pin the mantillas on top of our heads. The scarves covered our heads as prescribed by the convent, but far from Jackie Kennedy's stylish pillbox.

As I entered the chapel, I felt momentary comfort at being in the familiar surroundings of our high school chapel. Floating legless nuns praying in the chapel used to induce fear in me. But now, I was one of them.

As the nuns began the intonation, the beautiful monotone chanting of the Psalms quieted my restless stomach. Indeed, chanting the Divine Office would be a bright spot in this dimly lit world inside the convent.

We returned to our assigned seats in the refectory for the evening meal. Sitting in silence, I awaited Mother Monica to ring the bell to begin speaking. But she did not. She merely sat with eyes cast down. Mother Monica blessed herself, leading us in a slow, reverent recitation of grace: "Bless us, O Lord, and these thy gifts which we are about to receive from thy bounty through Christ our Lord. Amen." My family raced through the prayer

to begin eating, but in the novitiate, the prayer seemed to drag. After the blessing, a novice took the Bible from a small corner desk and read aloud from the Gospel of Mark.

After all, it was Sunday, the Lord's day. I sighed. I had so much to learn.

Finally, the food passed down the long tables. Mother Monica rang the bell as the signal to begin polite conversation.

After dinner and an hour of "recreation time," the clock in the community room rang nine times signaling bedtime. Along with the eight novices, we nine new postulants marched upstairs to our cells. The third floor dormitory flurried with young soon-to-be nuns banging their jugs and basins in pursuit of water. When we pulled the curtains around our beds, the metallic scraping reverberated throughout the dorm.

As my body sank into bed exhausted, the flimsy white curtains did little to mask the sounds of splashing and rinsing teeth. I tossed in the unfamiliar bed. Wondering what my family was doing at home shot a pang of homesickness through me. Sunday dinner would be over. Did Penny miss my help in the kitchen? Did Mom and Dad feel the loss? The tears began to flow. I grabbed a Kleenex from my drawer praying I could sleep through the night. "Where are you, God?"

Chapter 3

Conforming to the Convent

Dear Mom and Dad,

I've been here one week, and I miss you so much. I never knew how lonely I could be. It's so different in here than what I expected. I had been looking forward to seeing some of my high school nuns, but we never get to see the professed nuns unless it is a special holiday. We begin our college classes this week. How are Penny, Polly, Kristin, and Robbie? Give them a big hug from me. I miss you.

Love, Your number one,

Patty

"**A**ve Maria," the chorus rang out in the dorm as it did every day at five a.m. Startled, I bolted upright in bed and launched into praying my

Latin, "Hail Mary." Postulants and novices bustled about their morning dressing rituals, emerging from their cells. I missed my clock radio at home easing me into the day with lively Sixties tunes; instead, the screeching sounds of the metal curtain hangers and the banging of the water jugs formed the wake up call.

Since deciding what to wear and primping with worldly makeup and hairdos had been alleviated, we could get to chapel in fifteen minutes. We were permitted to leave the novitiate building only to go to chapel or the kitchen. When we did leave the novitiate, we were to maintain silence, walking directly without speaking to anyone.

In single file like a good line of kindergarten children, we marched into the chapel taking our assigned places in the stalls on the sides. Each stall consisted of a wooden seat facing the center of the chapel. When the time came to kneel, the nun could lift the folding bench to make room to kneel toward the front of the chapel. Professed nuns in their black veils—those who had taken permanent vows—occupied the center pews.

As a student in this chapel, I gazed at the stalls wondering what the nun life was like. I longed to know what nuns did for fun or what they ate. I hungered to know. Now on the inside, having a short taste of the nun life, I wondered if I might have been better off keeping the mystery behind the veil. To banish my doubt, I reminded myself that God chose me to be a nun. "Thy will be done," I prayed the Lord's Prayer, then added. "For you, I will strive to be a good nun."

Following fifteen minutes of silent mediation, the melodious chanting of Matins began. "Sing praises to the Lord, O you, his faithful ones, and give thanks to his holy name," the nuns on the right side of the chapel intoned.

"For his anger is but for a moment, his favor is for a lifetime," the left side of the chapel responded in plainsong.

During our first week, Mother Monica taught us about the Divine Office. Sometimes called the Liturgical Hours, the Divine Office was deemed the official prayer of the church. These antiphons and canticles were chanted in unison at designated times during the day: Matins at sunrise, Lauds at noon, Vespers at sunset before dinner, and Compline at night before retiring. Spanning the entire day, the prayers coincided with the daily activities of rising, working, eating, and sleeping.

"They are meant to praise the Lord throughout the twenty-four hours of the day," Mother Monica explained. Our life in the novitiate revolved around these hours. Other activities played deference to the recitation of the Divine Office. While the professed nuns taught at the order's schools during the day, the responsibility of this worship service rested with the postulants and novices.

I looked forward to chanting the Liturgical Hours of the Divine Office. Four times a day, my doubt and homesickness found solace in their comfort. Warding off the darkness of unhappiness, that rhythm of prayer sustained me as I struggled with accepting my decision to take on convent life in obedience to God's wishes.

"Weeping may linger for the night, but joy comes with the morning," the chorus sang. The loneliness I felt during the night ebbed with the dawn.

After morning mediation and the chanting of Matins came daily Mass at six a.m. Attending Mass brought some familiarity from my high school days back into my upturned life as a postulant. The sacristan lit the altar candles, and the priest began the accustomed ritual. The nuns prayed their responses, filling my heart with tranquility.

Because Fridays were considered a day of sacrifice, we abstained from eating meat. Mother Monica would not ring the bell for any conversation during meals either. The Grand Silence would extend through the meal. Fellow postulants Catherine and Barb rolled the meal cart into the refectory as we listened to a scriptural reading for the day. Catherine handed off the serving platter of fried eggs to be passed down the table. I skipped taking an egg, transferring the plate to Eileen on my left. I hated eggs. Mom could disguise them for me, scrambling them with bacon or smothering them with ketchup. But the convent eggs resembled rubber eyeballs.

"Ring-a-ling." Mother Monica's little bell interrupted the dishing up of the eggs. Each of us, our eyes at the floor, came to attention in reaction to the bell, ready for Mother Monica's pronouncement.

"Patty, why aren't you taking the eggs?"

"I don't like them, Mother. I never eat fried eggs." My voice wavered with tentative wording, and I wanted to hide under a rock.

Mother Monica's scolding voice shot out at the opportunity to make a point about being a good nun. "You must mortify your body. Put your body to death by not giving into the foods that it likes or dislike. Say 'yes' to your 'no' and 'no' to your 'yes.' We eat everything and are grateful for it."

Mother Monica pronounced each word with triumph. I know Mother Monica wanted to make me be a stronger nun. "But eggs?" I whimpered to myself.

She then added a final edict: "Pass the platter back to Patty."

My face reddened. I felt like I'd been hurled back into Sister Mary Cleopha's algebra class with humiliation crashing in on me.

Staring at the platter of fried eggs as tears rimmed my eyes, I plucked up my fork and lifted up the smallest fried egg on the platter. The stench of the cold oil nauseated me. To avoid any more attention directed my way, I put a piece of watery white into my mouth. It jiggled, and the crispy brown edge scratched my gums. I gagged. Gulping it down, I tried to avoid biting into it. A swig of water washed down the bite of the slimy egg, like choking down a pill.

Feeling Mother Monica's eyes crush in upon me, I forced myself through the remainder of the egg. Bite by bite, I struggled to keep from throwing up. When the Novice Mistress finally rang the bell, she diverted attention to the reading of the scripture. I gave a quick prayer of thanks for deflecting the eyes in the room from me.

But inside, I longed for my mother's cooking and understanding. Anxiety festered over Mother Monica's admonishment. With no camaraderie for support, no friends to vent my frustrations with, I turned to God for strength to endure her methods. I prayed for fortitude.

After breakfast, classes filled mornings and afternoons for the postulants. Mother Monica instructed us in religious life, and college professors from the outside came in to teach us regular freshman classes to prepare us to be teachers in one of the order's schools. Busying myself in studies occupied my mind, driving away the yearning for family and friends no longer in my life.

Two one-hour slots during the day were designated for recreation, one following tea and the other following dinner. Polite conversation was permitted for our social hour, but it lacked fun and heartfelt laughter. Without televisions, radios, magazines, newspapers, or other outside entertainment, we played board games with forced reserve and learned to crochet or knit.

"No, no, Patty. It's chain one and then double crochet," Sister Annunciata reminded me. The old fragile, stooped nun came to our recreation hours to teach us how to crochet. Looking pained, her curled arthritic hands demonstrated the skill while I fumbled to make the perfect sized loop for a pineapple doily.

Crocheting for recreation only widened the gap between the convent and home where physical outdoor activity like playing softball or swimming used more energy. My spirits dropped along with my activity level. I expected to live a more uplifting lifestyle in the convent, but found myself sinking physically and emotionally. Lying in bed, crying myself to sleep at night, I could hear cars circling the schoolyard honking their horns—my high school girlfriends coming to say "Hi." But I could not even go to the window to wave. Instead, I prayed harder.

After Mass one morning, we paraded back to the novitiate, mindful of The Grand Silence that forbade speaking from evening Compline until after Mass and breakfast the following day. As assigned for the week, Debbie and I dropped out of line stopping in the kitchen to pick up the breakfast cart to wheel to the novitiate.

Despite the Grand Silence intended to promote private meditation, Debbie prattled. "I can't find the butter. Do you know where it is, Patty?" She scrambled through the items on the shelf in the huge walk-in refrigerator.

"It's right here. I already have it on the cart," I whispered, trying to pretend that we weren't talking.

"I think…," Debbie broke off with a gasp. She stared over my shoulder, a startled look in her eyes. I whirled to face a deliveryman carrying a box of eggs into the kitchen.

"Good morning, ladies," he greeted us, walking toward the refrigerator.

I froze. With my mouth ajar like a gawky schoolgirl, my composure unraveled. We had been told never to talk to anyone, especially outsiders. These outsiders were from the materialistic world, and we were not to have any contact with them. Having left that world, we were to concentrate on the spiritual world. But I faced an outsider with my heart pounding in fear of what to do. To avoid being rude, I offered a simple "Good morning" in return with a quick glance.

Then, rolling the cart, I bolted from the room to dodge further contact with the outsider. I glanced back to see Debbie mesmerized. A sweet smile graced her face while the man unloaded the eggs in the refrigerator. I marveled at how demure she looked even though we broke two rules— speaking and mixing with outsiders.

I grabbed Debbie's arm, and we sped to the safety of the novitiate. Disguised under the noise of the wheels clanging on the tiled floor, Debbie reprimanded me in a loud whisper. "You know you're not suppose to talk to seculars. That's dangerous."

"I know. He started it. I was just being polite." Then I shot back, adding her crime. "You smiled at him. That's even worse."

Our banned conversation came to an abrupt end as we reached the refectory. We put on our silent masks as if nothing had happened and passed out the cereal, milk, toast, and butter. The assigned reader for the week began the life story of the saint for that day as the rest of us ate breakfast.

Wheeling the cart back to the kitchen in the convent as the black-veiled nuns left to teach, Debbie breathed a sigh of relief. "At least now we can talk legally."

As we turned to leave, she grabbed my arm with a sly smile. "Let's go into the professed nuns' refectory and see what it's like! It's empty in there, and no one will ever know."

"No way," I protested. We knew their dining room must be large with seating for more than a hundred nuns. Sometimes, while washing dishes in the kitchen, we'd catch a quick glimpse of the immense dining room through the serving counters.

"Oh, come on," she begged.

"Are you crazy? You know we're to go straight to the kitchen or chapel, nowhere else." I sensed the tightening of my stomach muscles just thinking how Mother Monica would react if we were caught snooping. We would be sent home. I wouldn't even think of such outlandish behavior in high school, much less in the novitiate.

"You're no fun," Debbie pouted.

"Guess you're right. I have always followed the rules," I apologized, dropping my head. But I didn't capitulate. I wanted to be a good nun, and I didn't want to be subjected to another admonition by Mother Monica.

In silence, we trotted back to the community room for our instruction time and slipped into our assigned seats. Mother Monica, standing like a statue, began her tutorial by capturing our eyes with her glare.

"Today, we are going to learn about an old monastic practice called "Custody of the Eyes," she began her daily lesson. "As a nun, you are in constant connection with God. Distractions, ever so minimal, could put that prayerful state in jeopardy." She paused to let her words sink in. I stared at her, bewildered at my apparent lack of religious prayerful state.

She continued delivering her lesson, pausing to peer intently into my eyes. I fidgeted, wondering if she knew about me breaking The Grand Silence with the deliveryman. Then, she demonstrated the Custody of the Eyes with her own posture as she articulated her explanation.

"Your eyes should be downcast and focused, not looking up," she pronounced, tilting her head to look at the floor. "It is not your place to be busy bodies noticing what is going on around you. 'Custody of the Eyes,' along with the rule of silence, should help you to listen when God is speaking to you."

My eyes flew to the ground. No doubt all the other postulant eyes did, too. I stared at the floor, feeling shame for my lack of discipline with the deliveryman.

When Mother Monica finished her instruction for the day, she dismissed the postulants to the vegetable pit to help the novices prepare lunch and dinner. As we started to leave the room, Mother Monica singled me out.

"Patty, may I see you in my office." Her voice commanded rather than requested my presence. My stomach twisted, and I felt like my heart would jump out of my body thinking that she knew I broke The Grand Silence with the secular deliveryman. As the rest of the postulants left to peel potatoes, I followed Mother Monica into her spartan office. She took her place behind her tidy desk while I slid into a chair to await my fate. Chewing on my lower lip, I tried to quiet my nerves while they raced in fear.

With her lips pinched together, she exhaled and launched into her speech. "Patty, I've read your letter home to your family."

My shoulders relaxed, and the unexpected topic of my parents soothed my jumping stomach. I breathed a sigh of relief, knowing I'd escaped chastising for talking to the man in the kitchen.

"The letter that you wrote home yesterday is much too sad to send to your parents. Your dad does not want to hear how lonely you are. That would only sadden him. You don't want to make him unhappy, do you?"

She probed my face to glean the smallest emotion. I dropped my eyes to the parquet to choke back the tears welling up. I missed my dad and mom. Even though I'd only been apart from them a short time, pangs of homesickness flailed every time I thought of them.

"No, I would never want to make them unhappy or displease them," I stammered, placating her with what she wanted to hear from a good nun. Slumping lower in my chair, I fought back the onslaught of tears. I couldn't say more lest my voice betray my utter loneliness.

"I knew you would feel that way. I want you to rewrite this letter with a happier tone, and then I will be able to send it on to your parents. Why don't you go out there now and quickly rewrite the note, and I'll put it in the mail today. I know they are anxious to hear from you."

Of course, Mother Monica was correct in thinking that my parents wouldn't want to hear of my unhappiness, but a deep sadness enveloped me. I longed to pour my heart out to my parents for comfort, but I had already learned that a good nun should think of others first rather than herself.

"God, help me," I prayed silently. "Help me not be so lonely, so I can be the best nun for you."

Taking the blank notepaper from Mother Monica's hand, I plodded out of her office with my shoulders drooping, wondering what to write to please Mother Monica and make my parents happy. Writing the truth wouldn't pass muster.

Dear Mom and Dad,

The weeks are flying by. I'm busy with my studies and doing just fine. Religious life is so peaceful. I hope everything is okay with you and the kids.

Love,

Patty

Secret One

Don't let religion get in the way of your relationship with God.

MY REFLECTION

Religion, intended to bring us closer to God, often gets in the way of our true relationship with God. Instead of taking personal responsibility for my search for pleasing God, I looked to the church, priests, and nuns to lead me to God—almost as if they were gods themselves. In trying to respect their authority, I gave away my power. While giving up my individual sense of worship, I mimed their words as prayers and based my actions on guilt. I allowed myself to be directed by an external prescriptive checklist, attending Mass, receiving the sacraments, confessing my sins, examining my conscience, reciting the rosary, aping prayers, and following rules. The practice of religion got in the way of my relationship with God, and I stumbled in looking for God in the church, rather than within me.

THE MORAL WE CAN ALL LEARN

Don't let ONE way be the ONLY way…with anything in life. When was the last time that you questioned the conventional way? Going against the norm may bring you growth and perhaps a better way. Free yourself of rigid requirements to be your own person, defining your own purpose, and trust your own power of discovery along the way. Others may have input, but you are responsible for your own growth. Recognize that ordained ministers and religious institutions are there for illumination and support, but not as the solitary path. Be open to finding spirituality as an all-inclusive journey not limited by prescribed rites, rituals, and rules of one church, one faith, or one belief system. Open yourself to the awesomeness of God wherever you look. That enables you to search guilt free for meaning and happiness.

Chapter 4

Submitting to My Superior

Dear Patty,

The holidays are approaching. We're enclosing a check for you to get something that you and the nuns would like. Wanted to let you know that IBM will be transferring Dad somewhere, probably San Diego. We're not sure of the date yet, but will let you know. We miss you and wish you could make the move with us.

Love,

Mom and Dad
XXOO

The envelope from my parents had been slit open. According to novitiate procedures, Mother Monica screened the letter. No secrets hid within the convent walls, personal mail included. Mother Monica knew what came into the convent walls to influence us and what went out as the reply, keeping all postulants and novices under constant surveillance.

I sat in the community room reading the much-awaited Sunday mail, the highlight of my week. Autumn's red and yellow leaves disintegrated into dried crumpled brown lifeless remains on the frozen ground, the withered shells reminding me of my own life. My once invigorating high school schedule had been usurped by the dull routine of cloistered studies, instruction in religious life, and prodigious manual labor. Letters from home brought the only joy into the daily regime.

"Oh, my God, they would never leave me, would they?" I panicked as my eyes raced over the letter informing me of my family's upcoming move to California. Not being able to talk to my parents, or see them whenever I wanted had been difficult enough. Just knowing that they lived across town gave me a sense of security. But that they would move thousands of miles away to California leaving me like an abandoned orphan in Nebraska! I felt sucker-punched. Had I not been seated, my legs would have collapsed, sending me sprawling like a newborn staggering calf. A new chord of loneliness descended around me. I skimmed the words again and again, hoping I'd misread them.

Reading the letter for the fourth time, I finally comprehended a sentence about Dad sending a check to me for the approaching Christmas. Not seeing an enclosed check, I made a mental note to ask Mother Monica about Dad's money and returned to staring at the words announcing my family's departure.

Seeking some support, I peeked around at my fellow postulants sitting in the community room in the small one-piece desks. Everyone poured over mail from home. Several postulants and novices already scrawled at their weekly responses. Most wore big grins on their faces in such contrast to gloom I felt.

Leaning over to Catherine who sat next to me engaged in a response to her family, I asked, "Whatever do you write about?" Topics that would pass Mother Monica's censorship stumped me, and this time, I had no idea what to write in response to the family moving to California. I couldn't tell them that I really felt that they were abandoning me.

"Shh, Patty, you know we're not supposed to talk until recreation time. I'm writing about the walk we took around the grounds and the beautiful gardens abounding with fall flowers," she whispered. Her eyes darted from her pen to the methodical observation of our superior, ever watching over us.

I could tell by her retreating body language that Catherine wanted to return to her letter writing. But I persisted in desperate need of a passable subject. "You mean last Thursday when we walked to the nuns' cemetery and ran into the high school girls?

She nodded, "Yes."

Perplexed, I slumped back in my seat. In contrast to the beauty Catherine saw, my version of the walk dripped with futility. Instead of a memory of fall flowers, I only recalled the cemetery with crosses for each buried nun. The simple white crosses conveyed the pointlessness of living and dying in the same spot. Something akin to a lifetime prison sentence. A life sentence by God.

I remembered the three high school girls we had spied hiding in the nuns' cemetery. The girls, who had cut class for a cigarette, chattered loudly, thinking they were secluded from sight. Their laughter drew a sharp contrast with how much my life had changed in three short months. For me, Mother Monica had mapped out my life following the required protocol of the nunnery, even to the dismal place of my burial. Despair wrapped around me.

I stared at my paper, longing to write about how much I missed my family, my friends, and my freedom. I could write about my perspective of the crosses, but Mother Monica would deem that too sad for my father to read. I could beg my family not to move to California without me. But that letter would never get stamped.

I stared at the desk, depression engulfing me. Reluctant, head drooped while my hand picked up the pen. This letter would be the last correspondence with my parents before Christmas. In the novitiate, we observed Advent—the four weeks preceding Christmas—with the cessation of receiving or sending of letters. My stomach cringed at the thought of the link to home being severed.

Foregoing correspondence was a sacrifice expected of a good nun.

Mother Monica said that the more difficult the sacrifice, the dearer to God we would become. Wistful images of our Advent wreath at home, bedecked with purple and pink candles, flitted through my head. Penny and I always fought over turns to light the tapers. We loved to spin the wreath around on the Lazy Susan—a delight that seemed so childish now in hindsight.

I sat in the community room pretending to write, staring at the blank page before me, but no words appeared on the paper. Waiting for inspiration, I gazed around the room. The other postulants bent over their desks, appearing to pour their hearts into their letters, but I could not muster the enthusiasm. That's when a realization hit me.

"Maybe I'm not supposed to be a nun. If I did have the special calling, I wouldn't be this miserable," I rationalized. The nuns that taught me in high school seemed so happy, but I didn't experience any of that joy. The convent seemed wrong for me.

I peered over at Judy, longing to talk to her about her decision to become a nun and how she felt now that we lived in the convent wearing the clunky nun shoes that we had purchased together. But Mother Monica had made it quite clear that Judy and I were not to be together, to seek each other out. First of all, the rules forbade being alone with another nun unsupervised. When we were supervised, we could only talk about certain approved topics; nothing that transpired behind those closed convent doors was to be discussed. The closest thing I had to a friend in the convent, much less a confidant, was Judy, and we weren't even permitted to talk.

I straightened up in my chair, steadying my breath. The strict rules of when to speak, with whom to talk, what topics to discuss, and where to converse cinched like the straps of a straight jacket to control the unruly. Contemplating my unhappiness, I pondered the notion of leaving the convent.

That night in bed, my thoughts filled with reasons why I should abandon my calling to be a nun. I worked backwards through the past several months—receiving lessons from Mother Monica, chanting in the chapel, treading silently through the halls, and entering the convent on my first day. One lonely image upon another. I thought back to the conversation on the back patio of our house when I told my parents that I wanted to be a nun, I was so sure of my calling.

"I'm not going to college. I want to enter the convent and become a nun."

I announced my intentions that bluntly. Time seemed to sprawl out languid in the heavy humid air while I felt my insides curl up, waiting for an answer. Riveted on my parents, I perched on the edge of the woven plastic chair. More silence.

Dad stared at me. I looked him straight back in the eyes. Now was not the time to back down. Mom looked away. Setting her cocktail glass on the small end table, she folded her hands with interlocking fingers almost in prayer. As usual, she draped herself with calm to show little emotion.

Dad, who carried the strong religious gene of the two, understood the complexity of the call from God. Converting to Catholicism for marriage sake, Mom lacked full comprehension of the special calling to be a nun.

"Well, Pat," Dad broke the silent standoff. "Your mother and I shouldn't be surprised that you would want to attain the highest form of dedication to God. But I don't know how I feel about this decision."

He stood to lecture me. "You are too young to make an important decision like this that will change your life forever. Why don't you first try college? After a year of school, then if you still want to be a nun, you could enter the convent."

I gave the appearance of pondering his suggestion, knowing full well that I would not and could not wait. Keeping my whole body alert and ready to enter into battle in case he had a change of mood, I listened to him talk about the maturity needed for this big step. Then I took a page from Mom's playbook, settled back, and folded my hands listening to his diatribe until Dad, pleased with his presentation, resumed his seat.

"Why should I put off the inevitable? God always has His way," I volleyed back. God's will would be a persuasive point with Dad, one he couldn't argue against. I pressed on, standing, grinding the point, in case he missed it. "What happiness would I ever find if I didn't do God's will? I want to go into the convent first. If I don't like it or God doesn't want me, I can always leave and go to college."

No one, not even Dad, could argue about God eventually winning and getting what or whom He wanted. I stared at him like an attorney before the jury. "That way we can see if God really wants me without my wasting a year of your money on college," I reasoned. Smug at my own sensibility, I plopped in my chair to await his reaction.

We all knew that our Heavenly Father trumped my earthly father. My decision weighed as my parents' obligation also. Giving back to God for His many blessings was a value that our family held dear.

With a forlorn voice, Dad relented, "You're right, Patty. It doesn't matter what we want. It's what God wants that matters. We are all here to do God's will. We were made for His divine purpose." Dad's shoulders caved in, and with remorseful eyes he gave in to the higher power.

"Thy will be done, on earth as it is in heaven," I reminded my parents of the words to the Lord's Prayer to reassure all of us that we were doing the right thing.

My parents looked into each other's eyes knowing they couldn't argue with God. They would sacrifice their first-born daughter to the church rather than walk her down the normal path of marriage and children. Although I won the argument, my heart broke looking at the loss written across

*their faces. The ice in their drinks clinked against the sides of
their glasses—the only sound breaking into the silence that
had fallen once more.*

Looking back at the conversation, Dad could have been right. As I wrestled in my bed with leaving the convent, I wondered if the devil tempted me with loneliness. The following morning, thoughts of leaving the convent still plagued me. I eyed Judy during World History class dying to ask her if she thought the devil could tempt me to leave, but I knew better than to talk. Struggling to keep my mind on my studies, I battled doubt of my calling and a strong desire to go home.

After morning class came the daily chores—washing dirty laundry, pressing wimples, polishing stainless steel sinks, waxing floors, peeling the vegetables for the daily meals, and cleaning the Motherhouse where the professed nuns lived. The refectory floor had been entrusted to me for the week, so I picked up the mop.

"Manual work keeps the mind free to listen to God," Mother Monica instructed in one of her frequent aphorisms.

But God hadn't been talking to me lately. As I went about my chore of sweeping, washing, and waxing the refectory floor, my mind sunk into misery at the chasm between the convent and happiness. Trapped between the two worlds of familiar secular life and strange religious practice, I trudged through the rest of the daily routine like a puppet manipulated by hidden strings.

As we sat down for tea with my eyes affixed downward, I noticed out of the corner of my eye that Debbie's place sat vacant. "Mother Monica is going to be angry with another one of Debbie's late arrivals," I patted myself mentally for being punctual. After blessing ourselves, we sat waiting for the bell to ring signaling conversation. The bell sat untouched in front of Mother Monica. Instead of ringing it, she stood to make an announcement. "Debbie left us this afternoon. She did not have a calling to serve God in the convent." She spoke as if she made a routine announcement.

Then, without further explanation, she sat down. Donning a flat expressionless face, Mother Monica reached for the bell indicating tea and conversation to commence as usual.

My thoughts flashed back to that morning in the kitchen when Debbie and I broke The Grand Silence and the rule forbidding speaking with seculars. I remembered her desire to trespass into the professed nuns dining room. Inside, I smiled at her energetic spirit of adventure, but agonized at her departure. Debbie had just disappeared. No good-bye, no explanation. She appeared to have been plucked out of the novitiate into thin air. I surveyed the faces in the room, questioning how could we go on as usual. My fellow postulants began passing tea treats and conversing, but not about what was uppermost in everyone's mind—why Debbie left.

As a good nun, I couldn't display my feelings. The Custody of the Eyes helped me manage my emotions undetected. I buried the war within somewhere deep while praise for the delicious cookies filled the room. The rest of the day hazed over with thoughts of Debbie. I marched through the motions of studying, chanting Vespers, dinner, recreation,

Compline, and finally, The Grand Silence. At last, I found stillness without having to summon the gumption to make simple polite conversation.

As I lay in bed, I missed the night sounds that usually came from Debbie's cell, the rustling of the sheets, the occasional cough, or the soft exhaling breath of a deep sleep. From Mother Monica's introduction that first day, I knew what city she hailed from and what school she attended. But I knew nothing about Debbie herself—what she liked, what she disliked, what made her happy, what scared her. We were forbidden to talk about those things.

Tossing on my bed, I sorted once again through the pangs of loneliness, the question of my calling to the convent, and the uncertainties of the religious lifestyle. I decided to tell Mother Monica in the morning that I, too, wanted to leave the convent to return home. Sleep came in restless interims.

"Ave Maria," I praised, waking with a renewed sense of wellbeing. During morning meditation, chanting of Matins, and the celebration of Mass, I fought the anxiety about the impending discussion with Mother Monica, but concentrated on images of living in my own home, eating

Mom's cooking, listening to music, sleeping in my own bed, and even fighting with Penny.

Having completed the morning breakfast chores, the other postulants ascended the flights of steps to the third floor to begin school. I lagged behind, beckoning Mother Monica aside. "Mother, may I please speak with you for a minute?"

Mother Monica surveyed me. Her piercing look searched my soul, scraping through the bowels of my being for glimpses of what I needed to discuss.

"Hurry along, Patty, or you will be late for class," she remanded me with her tense lips pressed together.

"I need to talk to you as soon as possible. It's very important," I added pleading with my eyes.

"Nothing is more important in religious life than punctuality and adherence to the rules. You're late," she berated me. "Now go to class, and I'll meet with you after lunch." She punctuated her words with a scolding glare.

My spirits deflated and shoulders sank. I pulled myself up the steps. Upon entering the classroom, my eyes fell to the floor as I offered an apology for my tardiness not befitting a good nun. Stinging from Mother Monica's rebuff, I composed a blank stare for the instructor, pretending to take notes.

During lunch, we listened to a spiritual reading about the life of renunciation as it applied to Advent. I couldn't listen. I couldn't eat. I only had one thing on my mind. Lunch dragged as my bouncing leg kept time to my racing nerves. To appease my slighted self, I flung silent accusations at the Novice Mistress: "She won't even look at me. She just sits there, going through her motions, not really even caring about me."

Following noon dishes, Mother Monica appeared in the doorway of our study hall. Her small stature seemed much bigger cloaked with her confidence. Her serious expression and stern eyes posed a barrier, but hurdling her to go home gave me courage.

Gliding over to my desk, careful not to disturb the others who were deep in their books, Mother Monica whispered in my ear, "Patty, I'll see you now."

Following close behind her, I marched into her office. She sat in her chair, the expressionless superior. I stood like a mouse facing a tiger. Focusing my eyes on the floor, I crossed my feet at my ankles; she crossed her arms waiting for me to begin. I finally capitulated, raising my eyes and blurting my words.

"Mother Monica, I don't think I have a calling to be a nun. My dad is being transferred, and my family is moving to California. I want to go home to be with them."

My heart pounded so loudly that I thought the whole convent could hear. With her eyes softening a bit, she dropped her arms to her sides and walked over close to me.

"You are one of us now, Patty."

"I know, Mother. But my family is moving, and I have to go with them."

"But we are your family now. You will have to let them go and focus your attention on learning to be a good nun."

"You are not my family," I shot back, dropping my eyes to the floor. I knew full well that I had overstepped by boundaries.

"Patty, I know this is difficult for you with your family moving, but God has given you a special calling to serve Him." Mother Monica mollified her tone. "You will have to suppress your moods and not give in to what your body and emotions are telling you. We live in the spirit. Just put on a happy face, and you will find joy in doing God's will." She modulated her words into soothing tones.

"You just don't understand." My insides burst as a sob rose.

"I understand," Mother Monica placated me, but her cool voice seemed devoid of any real comprehension. "You are just tired. You have had a trying day. Go up to your cell, go to bed, and you will feel better in the morning." Mother Monica's final words flipped into an order accompanied by a return to her flinty face.

Beaten down like a cowed animal, I obeyed. Crawling into bed at two o'clock in the afternoon, I sobbed through one box of Kleenex and slept through to the next day. I felt imprisoned in a world of total separation with no way out. Indeed, the novitiate felt like a penitentiary, and no court of appeal would release me from the dungeon.

I prayed for God's help. But no help came. Instead, I settled for chanting: "Thy will be done, thy will be done."

Chapter 5

Severing the Ties that Bind

Dear Mother Monica,

May I please have a box of Kleenex.

Thank you.

Patty

Trudging down from the third floor the following morning, I wrote on Mother Monica's notebook outside her room. I hoped my request didn't surpass my Kleenex quota.

Back in the routine, I participated in spiritual instruction and classes as if nothing had happened. The daily regimen served as an antidote for the agony that made me want to leave. An anesthetizing acceptance inched in its place. An acceptance that Mother Monica had a better pipeline to God than I did. She seemed to know that God still wanted me to be a nun despite my misgivings.

One day, I sat in English class taught by a nun from the local Catholic women's college. Mother Monica slid up to doorway floating with stealth, as if she were on a secret mission. She rarely interrupted classes, so her odd behavior raised my suspicion. Our eyes met as she raised her right arm, turning her palm upside down and beckoning me with her pointing finger curling in to say, "Come here."

My mind raced to guess why I had been singled out for removal from our class. I flipped through my most recent failures at being a good nun, searching for which ones warranted a disruption in the daily routine. Walking behind Mother Monica's limbless black form leading me to her office, I felt like she escorted me into the school principal for discipline. With my heart thumping, I sat facing her awaiting my fate. She sat unyielding behind the barrier of her desk, reflecting the height of religious decorum.

"Patty, I received a phone call yesterday from your parents." I sat like a stone to ward off panic in anticipation of bad news. Mother Monica's piercing blue eyes never flinched.

"You knew that there was a possibility that your father would be transferred with his job. IBM sent him to San Diego. Your family left this morning for California."

"What?" I wanted to scream, but the word tripped up in a sob. I slumped back against the chair for support. My loss reared up with a searing isolation. "They left without telling me? They disappeared without saying good-bye?"

"They called to say good-bye, and I reassured them that I would relay their message. We all know the rules about not talking to parents, especially during this sacrificial time of Advent."

Mother Monica lectured me about the Advent rules, but her words tumbled into incomprehensible white noise. She sat in her chair with all the prim appearances of the perfect nun. Aloof. I covered my face with my shaking hands to hide my tears.

"You will get to talk to them on Christmas day," Mother Monica offered after a long pause. A poor dollop of pacification for the heart-shattering news she'd just delivered.

I sat numb. Numb to my thoughts. Numb to everything. Only my loneliness sharpened to a point that drowned out all else. Mother Monica droned on while her words swirled through me.

"Patty, you are very attached to your family. This move will prove good for you. You need to put yourself aside and concentrate on doing

God's will. You are trying to detach yourself from the world you knew. Don't think about your loss, but put your energy toward fulfilling your daily responsibilities."

She didn't comprehend my loss. She sat, cold and uncaring. I wondered if she even had a family. Mother Monica tried to coach me with religious logic.

"Say 'yes' to God's call as the Blessed Virgin Mary did when the angel asked her to be the mother of Jesus. You, too, need to answer 'yes, be it done according to your word.' Go to the chapel and find peace in God's presence. I know you will feel better."

With those words, Mother Monica dismissed me. I left her office, my eyes red, my face teary, and my stomach lurching. Deserted by my family, I stumbled out of the novitiate toward the chapel, plodding one foot in front of the other, barely able to see through my tears.

In the quiet of the chapel, my panic subsided at the sight of the Pietà. That sculpture of Mary at the foot of the cross receiving the dead body of her son Jesus into her arms never failed to speak to me, even when I came to the chapel as a carefree student. This time, the Pietà calmed me as I felt Mary's pain. I was not the only one who suffered loss. Mary and I shared the loss of loved ones.

Peace descended on me in the chapel, subsiding the churning of my stomach. I had chosen to be a nun, and my family moved on without me. Maybe Mother Monica was right. Maybe I needed to detach myself from my family. Emotionally limp, alone, I had to follow the rules of the convent, just as Mother Monica ordered.

During the next couple of weeks during Advent, I threw myself into my college studies, prayed even harder, and read more about renunciation. I strove to leave the materialistic world behind to develop spiritually. Whenever images of my parents or my siblings snuck into my mind, I shoved them far from my consciousness. I forced myself to be dead to the world, even to those I loved.

About ten days before Christmas, when we plucked at our needlework during recreation one evening, Mother Monica interrupted our polite conversation. "I have some good news." Her face beamed with excitement in contrast to her normal guarded demeanor as she held up a LP record album cover. "A generous donor has given us a contribution to purchase this set of beautiful Christmas music."

She displayed a collection of four records entitled Handel's *Messiah*. "We can enjoy these right now because there is a selection for Advent and also one for Christmas," she described the music as she moved to the record player. Before the music started, she added, "You know that singing is like praying twice."

Mother Monica put the needle down on the vinyl record at the Advent piece, and melodious tender music softened the rigid atmosphere in the community room. In three months at the convent, I had not heard recorded music. Listening to music, which had once been a part of me like breathing in and breathing out, belonged to that materialistic world left behind. The classical melody sang so differently from my rock radio tunes, but the strong emotional score evoked a soothing gut reaction.

Musing about the anonymous donor of the Advent music caused a puzzle piece to fall into place. My dad had probably been the "generous donor" responsible for the music. My parents mentioned an enclosed check for Christmas in their last letter, but I never saw the check. It vanished from the envelope before I received it. Mother Monica never referred to the money my father sent. I felt duped on impulse, but buried the feeling as connected to the materialistic world. A good nun would be proud to have the money spent for everyone's enjoyment.

I had found success at pushing my family from my mind, but the music coupled with my dad as its source rubbed raw feelings of abandonment. The music rang with a longing I felt, the yearning tones welling up a craving to see my family. But I had ten days before I would be allowed to talk with them. With impatience, I counted the days.

As Christmas Eve midnight Mass arrived, we awoke to a chorus of singing that sounded like angels, "Come, come, come to the manger." As postulants and novices rushed to dress for the service, the professed nuns stood on the steps of the novitiate singing the most beautiful Christmas carols—their voices reverberating throughout the tiled hallways.

With the music's beauty, we forgot all about Custody of the Eyes, and we looked up smiling like wide-eyed tots waiting to see what Santa had in his bag. The angelic chorus shone with light flickering from the tapers they carried, the soft warm glowing candles replacing the harsh overhead lights. With the sacrificial season of Advent behind us, the songs heralded the arrival of the joyous Christmas.

The black-veiled nuns caroled with joy until we were ready. In line behind them, we all processed down the hallway into the chapel. Bedecked with bountiful red poinsettias, the chapel had transformed from the solemn house of prayer to a colorful sanctum bursting with exultation.

As I took my normal assigned seat in the stall on the chapel's side, midnight Mass blessed me with tranquility. The familiar reading of the Christmas gospel reinforced by the traditional Christmas carols dropped a blessed peacefulness into my aching soul. After the rending of my heart with my family's move to California, perhaps I had worked through that test from God and was ready to say, "yes" to God's invitation of dedication.

The angelic chorus of nuns awoke us again on Christmas morning, calling us to chapel to chant Matins. Usually the convent held no good surprises. Our days filled with dull routines allowing us the quiet to converse with God. But Christmas held delights.

Color from red poinsettias lit up the usually drab refectory. At my assigned seat sat a bundle of letters all tied up with a red bow. My heart quickened. The best Christmas gift ever sat on my plate! The pile had to be all the letters from home that had arrived during Advent. I could hardly wait to pour through each note.

Because of Christmas Day, our usual instruction time gave way to an extra hour of recreation—time we spent going through our accumulated mail and a few sparse packages. I read and re-read each letter, learning of my family's move to California with the details of the new house and adjustments to the new life. I couldn't wait to hear their voices on the phone that afternoon.

I spied a package for me showing a return address from Jackie, my best friend since sixth grade. Tearing at the brown packing paper, I dug into the box, wanting to reconnect our friendship. The box contained gloves, scarves, and mittens—accessories reminiscent of my past life.

My girlfriends that I dearly missed had assembled the items together as a care package. My heartstrings tugged thinking of the walls that now separated us. I glanced over at Judy, and she, too, opened a similar box from our friends.

Before we tried on the scarves and mittens, Mother Monica swooped in on Judy and then me, plucking up our boxes of Christmas gifts. Getting everyone's attention, she stood ramrod straight, her steely blue eyes sweeping the room.

"Thank you, Patty and Judy, for the warm mittens, scarves, and gloves. These are ours now. As you know, the vow of poverty that you are preparing yourselves for prescribes sharing with the community."

I didn't mind sharing my scarves and mittens, but I wondered if I'd see them again. Their disappearance into Mother Monica's possession reminded me that my friends lived in the materialistic world. My ties with them must sever just like the mittens disappearing.

Following a delicious prime rib dinner served at noon, the time finally arrived for phone calls and visitations. The few postulants and novices that had nearby families were allowed an hour with them, accompanied by Mother Monica.

Even on that day, my happiest day in religious life, I swung between jealousy and guilt. My feelings of abandonment raged thinking that my family should have come to visit, and envy in my eyes followed the postulants trotting off to hug their parents. Guilt battled the envy by bombarding me with Mother Monica's voice, "A good nun is happy for others. Jealousy is sinful." I sat with a heavy heart waiting to phone home.

After supervising the visitations, Mother Monica called me into her office and dialed my parents' new number in California. I tucked the receiver to my ear.

"Hello," Dad boomed, in his deep familiar bass voice with the Midwestern accent. My heart exploded when I heard his voice. But so much time had passed since I had talked to him that I fumbled with where to begin.

"Hi, Dad. Merry Christmas," I stammered.

"Merry Christmas to you, too. How are you, Patty? We miss you so much," Dad's voice quivered.

"Are you having a good Christmas?" I blurted, sounding like a silly schoolgirl to ward off tears. I berated myself for not planning exactly what I wanted to say.

"Did you get the money I sent for a Christmas gift?"

"Yes, Dad," I reassured him, glancing at Mother Monica out of the corner of my eye. "We all enjoyed the music of Handel's Messiah."

Mother Monica, supervising my phone call, offered an approving smile. I felt, for once, like I was being a good nun. "How's California?" I asked to make polite conversation, not really wanting to hear the details of their new lives without me.

"It's beautiful out here. Right now it's seventy-five degrees, warm and balmy. Doesn't even seem like Christmas without the snow," he prattled on. I contrasted my family's new location with the icy Omaha December.

Dad handed the phone to Mom. Excited to hear another familiar voice, I hung on Mom's words about where the kids were going to school and her new golf and bridge groups. Mom added that they had hired a Mexican nanny to help with the younger kids.

While Mother Monica evaluated every word, I fought against saying what I really thought: "Tell them. Tell them the letters about the happy days in the convent are lies. Share your true doubts about living this religious life. Now's your time to tell them." But knowing Mother Monica's expectations, I kept the trite banter going. We discussed daily schedules, but nothing that really mattered.

"Give all my sisters and new little brother a big hug from me. Tell them how much I miss all of you. I can't wait to see you this summer." I ended the conversation, fumbling through words and fighting tears.

I felt worse than ever. I had been so excited to visit with my family, but the conversations just gashed open wounds. When each parent spoke, the words tore like a band-aid off fresh new skin.

Hanging up the phone, I looked over to Mother Monica for help. I felt lost in loss. She gave me a prim smile that pronounced my loss as vain. Then, she dismissed me to join my fellow postulants having tea downstairs.

"You'll feel better later tonight when we get together with the nuns for recreation. Some of your old high school teachers are eager to see you," Mother Monica offered what she saw as encouragement. Even the thought of seeing some of my favorite teachers couldn't reach into the chasm of loneliness that gaped within me.

As a rule, professed nuns who had already taken their vows stayed out of the novitiate. The building had been designed to isolate the postulants and novices to ensure proper training and to restrict tainting from the outside world. Since I arrived, I had never seen a professed nun other than Mother Monica in the novitiate. But Christmas Day brought the convent's sisterhood together, with nuns visiting together.

I pushed the memory of my family from my mind to mingle with the nuns who taught me in elementary and high school. Their warm faces lifted my spirits as they inquired about my new life in the convent. Smiling faces—radiating with genuine happiness—gave me the affirmation that nuns were indeed joyful, in spite of what I saw day after day in the novitiate.

"Oh, my wonderful child," a voice rose above the others. I turned to see Sister Mary Cleopha, my dreaded former algebra and Latin teacher from high school. Her face glowing with love, she reached for my hand. Tentative, I responded with my hand, wondering if my eyes and ears played a trick on me with a Christmas miracle.

"Yes, it's me, Dora Dumbhead." I laughed to ease my nervousness joking about the name she called me during a bleak algebra lesson when I gave an incorrect answer.

"That was then, and now you are one of us." The Sister patted my hand.

The incongruity of her concern vexed me. I thought she hated me when I sat in her class. Sister Cleopha would have never called me a "wonderful child" in school. "What a difference a habit makes," I surmised.

Christmas evening, we continued our celebration by writing to family and friends. Feeling eager to write for once, I penned the perfunctory letter home, sharing the delightful details of Christmas in the convent. I knew both my parents and Mother Monica would like this one.

I spent most of my letter time writing to Jackie and my group of high school girlfriends thanking them for their generous gift box. I labored with each word to form the message with perfect penmanship. The muscles in my fingers tensed as I tried to make each loop in the letter exemplary.

Upon finishing the thank you note, I re-read the words. They sounded like someone else's letter. The handwriting didn't resemble my penmanship at all, and the thoughts seemed foreign and hollow.

Dear Jackie,

Thank you so much for all your thoughtful gifts. I relish each day in the convent. I wish you could experience all the peace that I have found doing God's will. Share the grace and peace of Christ with our mutual friends.

Your friend in Christ,

Patty

Chapter 6

Struggling for Survival

Dear Mom and Dad,

As this New Year begins, I'm making my annual resolutions. This task is much easier in the convent not worrying about "talking back to you" and other bad things I used to do. This year I'm going to try to accept what God sends me and listen to where He is leading me. I'll be the best nun ever. Hope you are enjoying sunny California.

Love,

Patty XXOO

As we put the Christmas season behind us, we returned to the routine of college classes, Mother Monica's instructional meetings, and housework. Some people in the world experience post holiday blues. But I never did because I looked forward to celebrating my birthday on January 26. Whatever I didn't receive for Christmas had usually been marked down in January, so I could count on my wish list being complete.

But birthday cake, presents, and parties—deemed celebrations of the outside world—were now part of my past life. As religious nuns, we celebrated our name days instead, the day designated by the church to honor that particular saint after whom we were named. My name, Patricia, came from St. Patrick; March 17 became my special day.

By January, the convent had shifted my values. Now, the idea of getting everything that I wanted seemed shallow. After all, gifts displayed materialism, and I really didn't need anything in the convent. I strived to focus instead on spiritual riches.

January 26th came and went with not a word spoken about that day being my special day. No one wished me "Happy Birthday." No one baked a birthday cake.

But ignoring my birthday seemed strange. I wondered if my parents remembered my birthday? I pushed the happy memories of past birthdays out of my mind, reminding myself that I was silly to get caught up in earthly cares and my past life.

Waves of homesickness waned. When they did roil their frothy pangs, I expunged every thought about my family or what might be going on in California from my mind. Whenever a memory swelled, I clutched the rosary in my pocket to take me to a more spiritual plane. Armed with tactics to banish emotion, I treaded water in survival mode to live through the long lonely days behind the convent walls.

I drifted on the waves rather than trying to swim upstream against the convent's current. Mother Monica managed the map directing me to safe harbors for a good nun. I jumped on her boat, throwing myself into my education and striving to please her.

Every February, the postulants learned the history of the order by presenting The Founders' Day Program in celebration of the order's establishment. Our order—The Sisters of Mary—was founded in England in 1852 and expanded to the United States in 1871. For the program, Liz suggested that we sing the songs from *The Sound of Music*, changing some of the wording to reflect our convent life.

Judy launched into one of everyone's favorite songs from the movie.

"Raindrops on roses and whiskers on kittens, bright copper kettles and warm woolen mittens, brown paper packages tied up with strings, these are a few of my favorite things," Judy crooned in imitation of Maria. The movie had swept the country in 1965. Our entire senior class had attended a special showing with our mothers. The smiling, singing nuns in the movie helped me feel better about my decision to enter the convent. My mother left the movie proud that her daughter would be like Julie Andrews, and if the nunnery didn't work out, a handsome man would sweep in to rescue her.

We scoured our daily routines for things from the convent that we could adapt into the song. "I'd like sharp potato peelers for the vegetables," Liz offered.

"What about more cutting boards in the vegetable pit?" Barb chimed in with another idea.

Soon, we completed a list of things that could be substituted into the song. After a couple of song rehearsals, the new words didn't sit right with me. Instead of a list of favorite things, the items sounded more like a wish list to make our lives easier. We didn't sign on as nuns to make our lives more comfortable.

"The song is great, but I think the lyrics kind of sound like we are complaining about things, like dull peelers," I broached my objections to the rest of the postulants.

Following some discussion, they agreed with me. The words conveyed a message too negative for our celebration. We opted to change them to favorite things that helped the Motherhouse run smoothly, such as clean linens, apple pies, and bright, shiny waxed floors. Mother Monica smiled at our decision.

In my attempt to excel at being a good nun, weeks rolled into months, loneliness ebbing and flowing, like the ocean. High spirits sank each month on family visiting days. Parents near enough to visit the convent came to see their daughters for one hour. My parents, living in California, couldn't justify the trip each month for such a short amount of contact. The separation wound, which I deemed healed, gouged open again with each visitation day. On those days, homesickness led to waves of anger. "How could my family leave me here alone?" I demanded of God.

When smiling, bubbly postulants and novices returned back to the community room to relate family news from the visits, I moped. "Why not me," I whined to myself. "Where are my parents when I need them?" Resentment simmered, testing my endurance.

On one visiting day, I plopped down in the community room to wait for the remaining novitiates to return. One postulant scooted toward me, leaning in to speak, despite the rule of silence.

"I'm so scared," Anne confided in a soft squeak. "I just saw Liz walking out the door with her parents. She was dressed in her street clothes, and her dad was carrying her suitcase. I think she has left the convent for good."

The news kicked me in the stomach. Another unexpected loss. Our group of nine postulants now dwindled by two girls.

"What happened?" I asked.

"I'm not sure. I thought that Liz would make it. She always tried to be a good nun."

From the very first day, tall, skinny, freaked-out Liz, couldn't remove the "Are you kidding me?" look of amazement from her face. Her eyes often appeared red from crying. I shouldn't have been so surprised that she would depart.

Mother Monica floated erect into the community room and sat with grace and confidence, eyes straight ahead. After calling our attention, she made the announcement.

"Liz will no longer be with us."

Silence. Subject closed.

That night, I tossed in bed trying to analyze why two girls left the convent. Did they choose to leave on their own or did Mother Monica find them unworthy candidates? And why did Mother Monica let Debbie and Liz depart, but not me? Questions marched through my head. But I found myself adrift without an answer.

By June, my spirits soared in anticipation of seeing my family during the annual permitted visit home for one week. As my plane set down in California, I could barely contain my joy at getting to be with my family. I so longed for warm hugs and my own things. To avoid having me transfer planes, the family drove from San Diego to Los Angeles to pick me up. Wearing my postulant black, I stepped off the plane.

"Pat," shouted a familiar male voice across the Los Angeles airport. "Over here."

I whirled to catch Dad, Mom, Penny, and Polly. Minus my two youngest siblings, the four rushed to greet me.

"Oh, it's so good to see you," Mom spouted, overflowing with unusual warmth.

I fought tears at seeing their beaming faces, but my nine months of religious training won out to maintain propriety. I stood, feeling awkward and uncomfortable, while they took turns hugging me with reserved affection. Something seemed forced and artificial, but I clung to the hope that our initial meeting in the public airport would give way to the warmth of home once we reached San Diego.

"We've been looking forward to your coming home for so long," Dad gushed, dabbing his eyes. I wanted to hug him, but fought to compose myself to avoid acting childish.

"If you only knew how much I missed you, too." My pent up emotion spurted out. "It seems like forever since I left. I couldn't wait to get back home." Despite trying to maintain the decorum of a nun, I fell into my father's arms clinging like a scared child.

"Do you have to wear that outfit the whole time you're here?" Penny interrupted with bold sarcasm. I glanced down at my black religious dress. Against the backdrop of colorful California styles, I resembled a poor refugee visiting from a third world country. People stared at me.

Embarrassed, my eyes plunged on instinct to the terminal floor, and I mumbled, "No, I can wear my own clothes when I get home." Then, to lighten the mood, I added, "That is…if I still fit into them. I've gained a few pounds, thanks to cake at tea everyday."

At the convent for the past nine months, the English afternoon custom of tea coupled with the lack of exercise put my once shapely body out of kilt. But admitting my weight gain broke the tension, garnering a polite laugh from everyone. I looked forward to lounging for the first time since September in my old jeans and T-shirts. As Dad led the way to the baggage claim area, I fretted that I really might not fit into my own old clothes.

Dad broke into my worry. "We thought that as long as we were in Los Angeles we should go do Disneyland today. How about that, Patty?"

"That would be wonderful," I gushed. Even at nineteen and a nun, I could still taste the anticipation of my childhood fantasy to go to Disneyland. En route to Disneyland, Penny, Polly, and I sat in the back seat, as usual, but nothing seemed usual about the drive. Traffic sped by, and cars honked. On fast four-lane freeways, expensive racers—shiny, showroom new cars like Porches and Corvettes—jockeyed for position. California seemed like a foreign country.

The peculiar surroundings, my disorientation, and my family's uneasiness caused forced intermittent conversations. Polly filled in the dead space by reading aloud restaurant and street signs. I hoped that once we got home to the house in San Diego, familiarity would comfort me.

Once in Mickey's world, disparity grew larger between my surroundings and me. Penny and Polly bounced to the amusement rides. But confined in religious garb, I felt like an alien on the sidelines, not filled with the excitement I expected. Maybe I had grown past Disneyland, past fun at nineteen years old.

At a food court, Mom and Dad gobbled down corn dogs and Cokes while I tried to figure out how to handle myself. The overdone fun park assaulted my senses. Scantily dressed girls bedecked with excessive make up pummeled my vision, and shouts of damning four-letter words battered my ears. Abhorrence rose in me like bile, painting my demeanor all the more like an outsider.

"Get a look at that outfit. Just another freak," one girl said loudly, drawing her friend's attention to me.

The words burned in my ears. But I forgave the mean comment with the excuse that she may have never seen a nun. I wondered why everyone got so excited about Disneyland and why I ever wanted to come to this Godforsaken arena so badly.

A colorful leaf on the ground caught my eye, and I snatched it up to show my parents. "Look, here is a stunning leaf that God made in His creation, and we're here all caught up in the materialistic world."

"That is a beautiful leaf, Patty," Dad concurred, wrinkling his brow in consternation. "Why don't you go enjoy yourself with your sisters? I know you've always wanted to come to Disneyland."

As I turned to locate Penny and Polly, I overheard Mom whisper to Dad. "She's weird, Ray. What happened to her?"

"Maybe I was weird," I thought. After all, I walked in the city of glitzy over–the-top movie stars, but dressed in my plain long black skirt, white long-sleeved blouse, black opaque tights, and nun shoes. My short, straight style-less haircut offset my shiny clean face devoid of even one stoke of makeup.

People stared at me. Since I hadn't really studied myself in a mirror for almost a year, I had no idea of what I really looked like. While in the convent surrounded by peers dressed the same with similar values, I fit in. But in Disneyland, I stuck out as a real mismatch. I wondered if I hadn't gone into the convent if I would have dressed like the girls at Disneyland.

As we drove home to San Diego, Penny and Polly recounted their electrifying day, ride after ride. I stared out the window, tired of listening to their glee at the worldly theatrics.

After we arrived at the ranch-style California house, a Mexican woman dashed to meet us carrying baby Robbie, now a one year old. Kristin, at three years old, bounced behind her.

"This is Sister Patty," Dad beamed as he introduced me to my own family and Laurie, the maid. Laurie's big gracious smile brought a grin to my own face. My shoulders relaxed, and finally, I breathed a sigh of relief to be home. But Kristin and Robbie shrank from me, not quite knowing what to think of Sister Patty.

Penny and Polly launched an eager tour of the house, beginning with the big living and dining rooms. They led me through Mom and Dad's spacious master bedroom with a sliding glass door out to the patio area. Penny and Polly shared a big bright room facing the front of the house with its circular driveway; Robbie's room tucked down the hall. We ended in the kitchen adjacent to the dining room.

"Where's my room?" I asked.

"Oh," Mom rushed to field my question. "You'll be staying in Laurie's room. Laurie is going back to Mexico to visit her family for the week. I put some of your clothes in her closet for you." The feeling of a lone outsider rose.

Mom led me down a narrow hallway at the back of the house to the maid's quarters. I inspected the room for all my belongings: my jeans,

T-shirts, skirts, and sweaters. My heart sank. Nothing looked familiar. "Mom, where are all my things, like all my other clothes and my stereo?" I tried to keep from screaming.

"We had to leave some of your things behind. We just couldn't bring everything from Omaha." Mom dropped her voice to a sheepish whisper, "Besides you are in the convent now and have no need of your old things."

"Some of my things!" Her words stung. Nothing of mine appeared to have made the trip to California. The gaudy palm-treed state, a house that wasn't my home, younger siblings who cowered from me, and a strange room usually occupied by the Mexican maid pinned me as an exiled wanderer. Nothing held familiar comfort.

I threw myself on the bed in misery. I had missed my family so much, but they made a life without me in California. I bit my lip, trying to staunch the tears. I remembered Mother Monica's teachings— that the materialistic world only drives people away from God. As nuns, we were to cut earthly ties. As I forced my body to relax, the little sobs retreated. I wouldn't let a few earthly items get in the way of my long-awaited visit with my family. I pulled myself together, forging ahead in religious stoicism.

The week flew by. The night before I had to leave to go back to Omaha, I found my favorite flower, a gardenia, on my pillow. Dad, in his own way, had tried to reach out to me. As I thought of the many things that I wanted to say to him, I knew I wouldn't say anything and settled instead for disappointment. The family didn't know how to react to me, and I played the good nun, never revealing any of my struggles over the winter in the convent. Dad wanted his daughter back, but the nun was not the same daughter any longer.

I had been so anxious to come home, but California wasn't home, and neither was the ranch house. With little of my things that defined my previous life, I belonged no place. The convent had become my only home.

At the airport the next day waiting for my plane to load, my parents and I sat with nothing to say. Their first-born daughter was now ill-matched with their new life in California. We felt the growing width of the grand chasm between us.

When I kissed my parents goodbye, a knife seemed to jab in my heart. I took it as sign from God. I was separating myself from my family, as Mother Monica recommended. I was shunning the materialistic world to serve God.

As I headed toward the jet way, Dad whispered to Mom, "We've lost her."

Secret Two

Life is not a matter of chance, but of choices we make along the way.

MY REFLECTION

Not finding the home that I remembered, I was blindsided by the feeling of estrangement. I didn't know where to go, so I took the path of least resistance, remaining a nun. Living with the status quo is a choice. Not making a decision is a decision. As I sat stuck in the quicksand of the status quo—not finding happiness at the convent, nor with my family—life passed me by. Day by day, I chose to succumb to guilt and tread water in place, which meant that I was choosing to remain in my present situation by not taking action. In the convent, the nuns referred to the behavior as "blind obedience," never questioning superiors. But I needed to take hold of the reins on my life, making choices for myself, to throw off the shackles of guilt that bound me to the status quo.

THE MORAL WE CAN ALL LEARN

Listen to your gut and make choices to avoid drifting into the clutches of the status quo. Ask yourself, "Is this where I want to be?" Be honest with yourself to answer the happiness questions. Some people try to "find themselves." But we don't "find ourselves," we "create" ourselves. Each choice defines our situation. If you don't like your situation—in a marriage, a job, or any kind of relationship—listen to your feelings and paint yourself into a new situation. The first step requires being truthful with yourself. Deep within the stillness of your soul, you will find answers. Give yourself time to reflect, assess, and face your feelings. The process won't happen overnight, but by being honest with yourself, you'll take the first step on the journey. Being honest with yourself will allow you to make the right choices along your life's journey and will allow you to live guilt free.

Chapter 7

Donning the Veil

Dear Mom and Dad,

Just think. It's been almost two months
since I've seen you, and soon, you will
come back to Omaha for my Clothing
Day ceremony. It's strange to think
that the last time you were here at the
convent began my life as a nun. Almost
a year has passed, and I'm ready to
take the veil to become a Bride of
Christ. Looking forward to seeing you.

Yours in Christ,

Patty

The long-awaited Clothing Day finally arrived in the August heat.
Knowing that my parents were on their way to the ceremony sent chills
down my sweaty body. Neatly folded stacks of black serge sat on each
bed in the dormitory. The virginal white veils symbolizing the state of
purity hung on the backs of the chairs. The new habits and veils awaited

donning for Clothing Day, the official step indicating formal acceptance into the order and our graduation from postulants to novices.

As I approached the mounds of black, I wondered how wearing the
habit would feel. Would it be heavy? Would the wool itch?

"Oh, my God," whispered Judy, taking in the piles of fabric. "Just
think. In a short time, we will be real nuns." Despite the rules of complete
silence in the dorm, Judy couldn't stifle the emotional rush that flowed
through the room. We'd looked forward to Clothing Day for a year.

The heap of ebony fabric looked mysterious. Expecting to see our
sister novices enter the dorm to help us learn how to assemble the habits,
I straightened when a strange nun entered instead, a comb and scissors
in her hands.

"My dear postulants," the Sister announced, "I have come here to
help you get ready for wearing your new veils. I'm sure that Mother
Monica has talked about the sin of pride being the basis for all sin.
Women's hair has been referred to as their 'crowning glory.' For this
reason, I am going to rid you of your glory and humble you for your
bridegroom, Christ himself."

I hoped the nun would cut my hair in a short bob—a style that I
once wore. The cropped cut would fit nicely under the veil.

With that prelude, utter silence descended in the dormitory. Eileen
took her seat in the chair set up as the barbershop. Clutching a shock of
Eileen's dark hair, the Sister attacked the tresses. But instead of stylishly
trimming them, she recklessly chopped them off short. Boyishly hacked
short. Brunette locks piled up on the floor.

Eileen sat stone-faced, like a little boy in abject pain at his first
dental visit. She read petrified horror in our faces—looks that told her
what she couldn't see. My stomach twisted in a knot, as I fought off
the urge to vomit at the demeaning of Eileen. My eyes affixed to the
linoleum floor for protection.

As I took the chair, I choked back tears. I tried not to listen to the
sharp blades hacking through my hair. I felt the Sister's cold fingers
randomly grab a wad of my hair and snatch the tangle between the
scissors. I read the revulsion on the faces of my fellow postulants as my
locks fell butchered to the floor. I closed my eyes, tight.

With all sense of pride and beauty stripped, we waited in shame for the novices to arrive, so we could cover our scalped heads. I gave thanks that no mirrors hung on the wall. Looking at each other was bad enough.

The novices arrived to help us into our habits and veils. Bouncing and ever smiling Sister Mary Bernadette, looking like she could break out with a lyric from *The Sound of Music* at any minute, came to help me dress for the ceremony.

"Can we start with the veil?" I rubbed my new butch haircut in humiliation. Without speaking a word, Sister Bernadette looked at me, her soft reassuring eyes full of consolation.

"We'll start with the tunic," the Sister instructed instead. She lifted the biggest piece of dark fabric from the pile, a long robe-like gown to put on over my head. My arms labored from the weight of the pitch-black worsted wool. The fabric rubbed like rough sandpaper on my palms, and the voluminous material felt like a tent draping over me. Poking my head out into the daylight, I rummaged around in the roomy frock for arm holes. Contrary to brides in white, no "fitting" was needed for a nun's habit.

"Cinch the black belt at the waist. That will adjust the bulk of the remaining material," Sister Bernadette said, pulling some of the coarse textile to drape over the belt. I remember Mother Monica teaching us that this belt or cincture was a sign of obedience. It was symbolically similar to a yoke put around the necks of the oxen to keep them together for the common good, each giving up their free will.

Trying to divert my mind from my hair, I recalled Mother Monica's explanation of the meaning of all the pieces of the habit as I donned each. The simple, modest habit reflected the dress of the poor peasant women of England in the1850s when our order had been founded.

Taking the coal-colored scapular from Sister Bernadette, I slipped the long piece of serge over my head to be worn over the tunic. The scapular, designed for manual labor, looked like a long apron. Hanging loosely over my shoulders, it fell to the hem of the tunic, both at floor length. My nose twitched as I breathed in the musty woven fabric.

With the Sister's help, I snapped the white starched wimple around my neck. It felt like hands choking my throat. I tugged to loosen its strangle hold. Secured in place, the cardboard stiff wimple gave me the appearance of wearing a bib. Every time I swallowed, my larynx pushed up against the confining wimple that seemed to have the strength of marble.

Last, Sister Bernadette took the snowy white headpiece and positioned it on my head. The headpiece symbolized my complete submission to God, and the chaste white veil would announce my purity from afar. After Sister Bernadette tied the veil behind my head at the nape of my neck, my neck muscles strained to support the heavy veil assemblage. The veil protruded out so far that it cut off all peripheral vision. I had to crane my whole neck sideways to glance left or right.

To complete the habit, Sister Bernadette took the large industrialized rosary, slipped it through the belt, and rearranged the beads so they hung properly. I glanced around the dormitory catching sight of the other postulants moving stiffly, like their joints were glued together, trying to adjust their gait to walking in the new habit.

As I dressed, I wondered when my parents had flown in and where they were staying. My first sight of them would be in the chapel amid many other anxious families awaiting their daughters' entrance. I wondered if they would have difficulty picking me out of the novices with only our faces as differentiation. As we moved toward the chapel, we looked identical in our stark somber black habits and unsullied white religious veils.

In contrast, the chapel radiated with color. Sweet smelling yellow roses and stargazer lilies adorned the altar. Crimson reds, bright yellows, and ocean blues bejeweled the congregation in the chapel. Fancy dresses, wide brimmed hats, Sunday best suits, and ties pronounced finery fit for any wedding.

The humid, sweltering August afternoon failed to put a damper on the celebration to signify our acceptance into the order as Brides of Christ. Families and friends crowded into the pews to witness their beloved daughters forsaking all else in marriage to Christ.

"Sal-ve, Sal-ve, Salve Regina," the choir of nuns exuberantly sang out as the Bishop led our procession of new novices into to nave of the church. Similar to a traditional wedding, the crowd stood turned toward the back of the chapel craning to catch the first glimpse of their daughters walking down the aisle. With a slow step, we marched in our new religious garb toward the altar for our religious marriage to God.

We had rehearsed this procession, but never realized how much different the actual event would be. With each beat of my heart, ecstasy pumped through my veins. Emotions clustered in my throat. My hands remained folded under the scapular as instructed, but my eyes could not remain downcast. I had to look up to find my parents.

I spotted them in an instant—in the same pew where they liked to sit for Sunday Mass. With her hands down by her waist, Mom gave me a little wave. Dad dabbed his eyes and tried to manage a smile. I choked back tears.

My sneaking glance met the watery eyes of other parents searching for the faces of their daughters. Some parents beamed; those with drawn faces reflected the dashing of long-held visions that their precious baby girl would walk down the aisle in white to marry a man. Like my father, they glowed with pride at their daughters' accomplishment, but at the same time juggled the loss sealed by the wearing of the habit. The habit represented one step further from family life.

Having made our way down the aisle, we knelt at the altar railing to begin the ceremony. The Bishop stood in front of us.

"My daughters in Christ, what is it that you seek?"

"The holy habit of religion and the help of Divine grace," we replied in unison.

As the Bishop sprinkled holy water on us and our new habits, he prayed that these clothes be blessed and preserve us in the state of holy religion. "Receive and wear these habits as a sign of your consecration to your Almighty God. Through self sacrifice, clear out your old self to make a more perfect union with Christ, your Bridegroom."

Near the end of the ceremony, the Bishop laid his hands on each of our heads giving us our new religious names. With a pounding heart, I waited to feel the pressure of his holy hands atop my veil and his announcement of the name that I would be called from then on. The weight of his hands pressed on my headpiece.

"Now that you are a Bride of Christ and have left the secular world behind, you, Patricia, you will be known as Sister Mary Kateri."

I flinched, recognizing a scarcely known saint by the name. None of us had any idea of the name we would be given. Mystery surrounded how our names were chosen for us.

"Ave, Ave, Ave Maria," the chorus rang as the Bishop led our procession out of the chapel.

With the new name Sister Mary Kateri, I waited for my parents in the garden for the reception. Sitting in a circle of white plastic rented lawn chairs, I fidgeted with my cumbersome veil, trying to find a pleasing position. The once much-hated ugly black nun shoes were the only comfortable part of me now. With the weight of the habit, I felt like I had trudged through hip high snow just to get outside. The nuns, legs hidden, seemed to walk so effortlessly in the long habits, like floating. I wondered if I would ever be able to glide as smooth as they.

When I spotted my parents, my religious decorum flew from me. I tried to run to them, but my feet, tangling in the hem of the tunic, almost hurled me to the ground.

"Mom, Dad, over here," I shouted. We gave each other awkward hugs, working around the intrusion of the headpiece.

"We are so proud of you, Pat," my Dad gushed, as the three of us sat down in the chairs—chairs no doubt used last at a normal wedding reception. With my parents flanking either side of me, my headpiece forced me to turn my entire head to catch their eyes during the conversation, action akin to watching a ping-pong match with the side-to-side motion. Wearying of the difficulty, I shifted my chair right in front of them.

"That's much easier on the neck," I explained, hoping that my words didn't sound like a complaint. I sidled into discussing my new name. "Dad, I know you're proud of me. And now I'm Sister Mary Kateri."

"Who is Saint Kateri?" my Mother asked. "I've never heard of her."

"Oh, she's actually not a saint yet, Mom." I hoped that she wouldn't ask too many questions about my new namesake, as I didn't know a whole lot about the saint.

"Kateri is Blessed Kateri Tekakwitha. She was a seventeenth-century Iroquois woman who dedicated herself to living a Christian life at an early age. That's about all I know about her. After some miracles, she will be canonized a saint." Mom seemed satisfied about Kateri's credible holiness.

"I like the name. It's kind of cute. It reminds me of Kristin," my Dad reflected, a momentary sadness at the changing family flickering through his eyes.

With the mention of Kristin's name, Mom opened her purse to pull out an envelope with a few pictures of my siblings. "I brought a few extra photos of Robbie because he has changed so much since you've seen him a couple of months ago," Mom shoved the pictures of her long-awaited baby boy in front of me. A broad smile spread across her face.

I perused the pictures as my heart felt a tug of pain. I chided myself, remembering that I had moved on and now had a new family of sisters.

"Oh, did you hear the name that Eileen received?" I said, pulling the conversation away from the loss of my family and handing the photo back to Mom. "You remember me talking about Eileen. She's from Detroit and her older sister named Sister Mary Faith was a novice last year. Now, Eileen's new religious name is Sister Mary Hope."

"That's funny. First Faith, now Hope, what next?" Dad lightened the mood. We enjoyed polite laughter as Mother Monica came to announce the serving of refreshments.

"Doesn't Sister Mary Kateri look well?" Mother Monica fished for positive comments from my parents.

"I have to admit that Patty, well…, I mean Sister Mary Kateri looks healthy and happy," Dad confirmed what she wanted to hear, his brown eyes glowing with pride.

"Help yourself to cake and iced tea on the porch. We have a special wedding cake for the occasion," Mother Monica boasted with her prim little smile, like a proud hen.

As Mother Monica floated over to another circle of celebratory families, I took the opportunity to educate my parents on the day's past tradition. "Mother Monica said that in previous years, the new novices like us processed down the aisle wearing real wedding dresses, complete with high heels. After the Bishop blessed the piles of habits, the postulants would take their new garb and return to the chapel in their new habits."

"That would be kind of strange," my Dad mused, "seeing you in a bridal dress one minute and then as a nun the next. That's quite the switch."

"I'm certainly glad that we didn't have to parade down that aisle in heels. It's been over a year wearing these nun shoes, but I've grown to like the comfort. I probably would have broken my ankle before I got to the altar."

Dad missed the point that today I was really a bride, a Bride of Christ. Instead, he chose not to acknowledge that he had given me away to the convent a year ago just like fathers do at the altar. If he knew it, he buried it deep inside.

Covering up the old girl—the old Patty—with new clothes and a new name, I took on the new persona of Sister Mary Kateri. As Sister Mary Kateri, I swelled with pride to look like a real nun. Garbed in the religious habit and vested in the cult of the black and white, I began my life of consecration as a Bride of Christ.

Chapter 8

Aspiring to Perfection

Dear Mom and Dad,

Thanks for making the long journey for my Clothing Day ceremony. Now I am beginning the novice year, our cloister year. We'll be isolated from the world so nothing can pose any distraction to growing in the three vows of poverty, chastity and obedience. This year will be more austere in hopes that we can die to ourselves to let Christ live in us as worthy religious Brides of Christ. Love to all.

Yours in Christ,

Sister Mary Kateri

"**P**erfection, sisters. Perfection and nothing less is demanded in your demeanor as a nun," Mother Monica prepared us for our next instruction. "You will participate today in The Chapter of Faults."

I had no idea what awaited us with the Chapter of Faults. Rules forbade discussing anything that went on in the seclusion of the convent with anyone, including each other, so not one of the novices the previous year let us know about The Chapter of Faults.

"The Chapter of Faults is derived from a chapter in the rule book that guides us in our religious development," the Novice Mistress continued. "You will be corrected for any infraction against the community rules and receive a prescribed penance."

I had been to confession before, but only in private to a priest. Maybe the Chapter of Faults would be similar. I honed in on Mother Monica's words to understand what would be required.

Mother Monica instructed us on the procedure. We needed to reflect on the past week and publicly confess our religious faults that may have led to the disedification of our fellow sisters.

I mulled through the past week, which seemed uneventful like every other week. I considered my actions, scrutinizing ones that may have stood in the way of my holiness and devotion. During our novice year, all of our secular college classes were postponed with the intent that our lives be dedicated solely to growing in religious sanctity. Our weeks filled with religious training, leaving little fodder from which to pluck faults.

Any infraction of the rules had to be admitted in the Chapter of Faults to receive penance. Mother Monica gave us a verbal formula for accusing ourselves in front of each other, similar to going to confession with a priest.

Uneasiness settled into my stomach as I tried to quiet my fears, reminding myself that all the other sisters would be sharing their warts also. As I stared at the floor demonstrating Custody of the Eyes, I tried to downplay the confession, figuring that none of our faults would be that horrific since we lived in the holiness of the convent.

The downed shades on the community room windows produced an eclipse of sunlight around the sill while the darkened mid-day room lent an eerie atmosphere. The absolute silence seemed more deafening than usual. As the new crop of postulants buried themselves in classes upstairs, Mother Monica led us novices with stealth into our first

Chapter of Faults. Like programmed robots, we filed in to take our cold seats in two lines of chairs facing each other, but following Custody of the Eyes, we never looked up to see each other. Mother Monica, as judge and jury, lorded over us in the head chair.

We sat, knees pinched together with flat feet, hands folded under our scapulars. In stoic silence wrought with tension and anxiety, we awaited our confessions. Blank staring downcast eyes, revealing nothing but empty shells of once vibrant teens, withdrew to a place unknown. Mother Monica broke the silence that held a palpable terror.

"Come, O Holy Spirit. Fill us with your light and truth. Wash us clean of our faults, so we may serve Thee in holiness. Amen."

Mother Monica concluded with her frigid blue eyes focusing on a pinpoint in the floor ahead of her. "You may begin your accusations, sisters, beginning on my right," she gave the directive to start the Chapter of Faults.

My insides tightened, sending spears of fear through me as Sister Mary Hope stood to plod her way to the center of the two rows of chairs. Kneeling on the floor facing Mother Monica, Sister Mary Hope sputtered as she spoke the rehearsed prescription while maintaining Custody of the Eyes, staring at the floor.

"I accuse myself to you, my dear Mother Monica, and to you, my sisters, of breaking the rule of religious modesty by walking too noisily and letting the door slam."

"Is that all, Sister?" Mother Monica pried, seeking more self-indictment from the trembling novice kneeling before her.

Nodding that she understood, Sister Mary Hope continued, "I also accuse myself of breaking the spirit of poverty by not referring to the toothbrush as 'ours.'"

"For your fault against religious modesty and poverty, you will say five Hail Marys for the souls in purgatory," Mother Monica reprimanded Sister Mary Hope.

"Thank you, Mother," responded Sister Mary Hope. She kissed her scapular as a sign of penance and returned to the line up maintaining strict Custody of the Eyes.

I reminded myself that the confession of our faults was God's way and that Mother Monica spoke for God. Our hurt feelings didn't matter. As novices, we needed to be tested and learn to rise above wounded feelings.

When my turn came, I rehearsed the confession of my faults in my head while I walked to the middle of the room. My chest tightened as my boney knees hit the unforgiving floor to kneel with humbleness before the Mother. I gave silent thanks for the Custody of the Eyes. No one would be staring at me, and my eyes were glued to the floor. I squeaked in a high pitch that sounded far from my normal tone.

"I accuse myself of breaking the rule of silence by speaking in the dormitory. I also accuse myself of disobedience of the rule of punctuality by arriving late for class."

"Is there anything else, Sister?" Mother Monica scrutinized me.

Rerunning my faults again through my mind, but anxious to get out of the hot seat and back to my chair, I shot out a fast answer. "No, Mother."

"Well, Sister Mary Kateri, you have been most lenient with yourself."

I strained to summon her meaning as her condemnation tumbled onto me. My stomach roiled. How had I had been lenient with myself? But before any answer came to mind, Mother Monica's voice thundered above me.

"I would accuse you of the sin against pride and vanity when you looked for your own reflection in the glass door on the cabinets in the refectory. You are very vain about your appearance. At one time, people may have cared about what you looked like, but not any more. Wipe that self-serving vanity from your soul. For your penance, go to the chapel and say five Our Fathers with your arms outstretched, praying for forgiveness."

Mortified, I opened my mouth to utter the final words of the prescription and moved my arms to push myself upright to return to my seat. But the Mother interrupted my movement with a further command.

"You may kiss the floor to humble yourself before us. Then return to your seat."

"Thank you, Mother," I eked out in a strangled voice. I folded at my waist and bent down to kiss the hard wood floor, stifling the tears that welled up. My lips met with floor grit as I obeyed my superior. Unfolding myself, I wobbled up from kneeling, thankful I could hide my tears under the headpiece. My legs quivered as I stumbled back to collapse into my seat. I wanted to wipe my lips, but dared not, for fear the Mother would call me out again.

When the last of the novices had accused themselves, Mother Monica recited a closing prayer, and the Chapter of Faults ended for that week. We rose, replacing the chairs in their normal positions, careful not to make eye contact with one another.

Lingering humiliation flared into my cheeks as I aligned the chair in its former place. Mother Monica had rebuked the others for breaking the rules, but she had attacked me personally. I fought to maintain my religious decorum by walking rather than scurrying to the chapel to perform my penance before mealtime. As I entered the house of prayer, which usually offered me comfort, I made my way to the middle of the chapel and knelt. Resting my head my in my hands, I hid my tear-stained face, praying for strength and humility to defeat my vanity. I sought consolation from the stillness hoping to feel comfort from God.

None came.

One day in late spring during our recreation, Mother Monica's sharp voice cut through the quiet of the community room as we sewed and crocheted. "Sisters! I notice the roving eyes of some of you looking out the window."

I snapped my eyes from the green elm trees outside to the wooden floor. Crimson shot up my cheeks. Lately, I had been sneaking glances out the window to see the world outside bursting with a spectrum of spring color. The rank air inside the novitiate made me long for the fresh garden scents to fill my lungs.

"Breaking the rule of Custody of the Eyes is very unreligious," Mother Monica lectured. "You must close your eyes to the allure of the outside world to avoid temptation. Avert your eyes from the salacious enticements of the world that would pull you away from our religious focus."

I forced my eyes on my crocheting, winding the yarn around the needle. Although I longed to be outside in God's creation, I kept my eyes locked on my crocheting to avoid another verbal lashing from Mother Monica. To occupy my mind, I threw my thoughts forward to August, when we would receive the black veil of the professed nuns, marking the end of our training as novices. Our original band of nine had now dropped to six, with a third novice opting to leave for a more contemplative convent. Sadness had enveloped me with the loss of another sister and all the unanswered questions surrounding the departure of each.

But after I looped only five more crochet stitches, Mother Monica's voice cut through the room again. This time, a strain frayed her usual overconfidence. "There is one more announcement."

"What else could there be," I thought, wanting to glance around the room, but staring at the floor instead.

"In the spirit of the Second Vatican Council, the present postulants will keep their baptismal names when they receive the habit as new novices this August. No longer will any nuns be known by different names other than their own birth names," Mother Monica announced. She continued to dictate the workings of the new edict: "The professed nuns will have the option of returning to their own birth names. The choice is up to each nun. Each of you novices will return to your baptismal names on the day of your profession of vows."

"I'll be Sister Mary Patricia instead of Sister Mary Kateri," I thought. My lips flickered into a grin. Even with the pride I felt at getting a new name on Clothing Day, the thought of returning to my birth name tweaked something inside me. Sister Mary Patricia fit me better than Sister Mary Kateri.

Little gasps of delight traveled around the circle of nuns, in anticipation of returning to using our real names. Sitting in all my high school classes, I often wondered what the nuns' real names were, instead of Sister Mary Cleopha or Sister Mary Michaeleen.

Then all of our eyes rotated to the postulant, Gina. Gina's older sisters were also in our order: Sister Mary Faith, one year ahead of us, and my fellow novice, Sister Mary Hope. Gina, along with everyone else, knew that she would make the trio complete, Sister Mary Charity. With this new ruling, we would no longer have Sisters Mary Faith, Hope, and Charity.

The official changing of our names occurred on Profession Day—the day we professed our temporary vows of poverty, chastity and obedience. Although the ceremony had more significance than Clothing Day, it paled in drama to being accepted into the order and being garbed in the religious habit. Profession Day, steeped in symbolism, celebrated our death to the world. Our clothing would now match the older nuns with black veils.

Our whole two-year training program in the novitiate prepared us for this graduation day. After studying the vows, we would publicly profess the promises of poverty, chastity, and obedience during the Profession Ceremony. We would receive the black veil as a mark of being accepted into the order as a real nun who has committed to live the three vows. From then on, we would be able to prepare for our mission of teaching by returning to the secular world to attend college, mixing with outsiders. These vows, considered temporary, applied to the next three years, after which we would renew our vows for two more years, before we would take our final vows to be nuns for life.

Profession Day also marked the final official relinquishment of my family, the total surrender to the church. I felt ready. I wanted to move on to become a full nun and pursue the work for which God chose me. My parents returned to Omaha to watch the ceremony. As I advanced to the front of the chapel to kneel in submission, I tried not to dwell on my parents and the symbolic death of my family.

After music accompanied the long procession of nuns into the chapel, we six surviving novices knelt in a line before the altar ready to declare our intent to renounce all worldly love. Each of us, in turn, pronounced total forsaking of earthly pleasures.

With a bowed head, kneeling, and eyes cast downward, I took my oath. I professed the vows of poverty, chastity, and obedience. Before God and family, I declared that I would live in a community owning nothing of my own, that I would deny myself the love and sexual relationship with a man, and that I would yield my will in blind obedience to the will and wishes of my superiors. I declared my vows with all of my heart, ready to serve God.

With those solemn words of declaration ending with "So help me God," black-veiled nuns stood behind each novice to assist us. Their fervent fingers untied our white novice bridal veils, replacing them with the sign of complete consecration—the black veil, which symbolized our extinction as an individual in the world. Lightning fast, with simple words of a promise and a swap to a black headpiece, I was now a real nun.

To complete the full symbolic submission, each novice prostrated herself laying face down on the floor. In the center of the sanctuary, the six of us lay in total surrender with arms extended, imitating Christ on the cross. As I buried my face in the dusty smell of the oriental rug on that humid afternoon in August 1967, I remembered that in past years at this point in the ceremony, the funeral pall of heavy black material would be laid over the nuns to signify the nun's death—death to the world and pledging to a life of sacrifice. I whispered a prayer of thanksgiving that Vatican II discarded that practice. The vision of death would have put my dad over the edge. I sensed him sobbing as it was.

As I lay face down on the carpet, while prayers were offered for our perseverance and strength, I pondered my life to come as a nun. As junior professed nuns the coming year, we would return to our schooling at a local Catholic women's college, preparing ourselves to be sent to one of our mission schools to teach one day. With the formal training of the novitiate behind me, I looked forward to re-entering the world as a consecrated nun, now Sister Mary Patricia.

I rose from the carpet with renewed vigor. I'd taken my vows to reaffirm my service as a Bride of Christ. With the same drive to please my family and the nuns in high school, I knew I would strive as hard as possible to live my vows and serve God to the best of my abilities.

Secret Three

"You can't steal second base until you take your foot off first." —Frederick B. Wilcox

MY REFLECTION

Pronouncing the vows in front of God and man securely fastened my foot with "guilt glue" to first base. Guilt—the ties of responsibility and not wanting to disappoint my Heavenly Father, earthly father, family, or my convent superiors—bonded me to religious life. I did not want to let them down by pursuing my own selfish interests. Locked in a fearful stance, guilt kept me bound to first base. I felt those pangs from that divine part of me that shares the spirit of God—but refused to give them credence. As a result, I clung to the safety of the status quo, unable to move on to second base.

THE MORAL WE CAN ALL LEARN

Challenge your status quo by asking the hard questions about your own happiness: Am I stuck in a job or relationship because I'm trying to please others? Am I parroting what others want to hear? Am I quickly justifying that "everything is just fine?" If you answer "yes" to these questions, it's time to peek under the veil of your answers. Dig down to your deepest emotions to discover the VIBES, the Voices of Intentional Beckoning Emotions. Your inner intentions reveal themselves in your emotions. These emotions are a true test for the heart's yearnings. Following those vibes will help you take your foot off first base on your way to happiness.

Chapter 9

Breaking the Religious Barrier

The clanging of our rosary beads against the metal frame of the car reverberated like splashing rain as we six new junior professed nuns piled into the Volkswagen bus to begin school in September. Not accustomed to the extra height with the veil, I knocked my headpiece askew as I scooted into the vehicle with my attention on trying to avoid tripping over my long skirt and heavy black mantle. I plopped my books down on the bench seat next to me as Sister Mary Judith started the engine, and we drove off to the all women's Catholic college across town.

As waves of social unrest swept through universities in 1968, my days passed cloistered between the religious life at the convent and instruction among girls at the church-affiliated college. Even my limited time spent outside the convent walls attending classes sheltered me from the counterculture revolution rocking the country.

Only bits of current world news trickled into the convent's heavy doors. Brief mentions of a war that had no actual beginning for me filtered through the monitored news broadcasts on television. As a high school teen, I remembered our country's limited involvement in Vietnam, but the small isolated scrimmage mutated into a world war that left me ignorant of its machinations.

Permitted a small television in the main convent, we huddled around the screen watching a world that seemed foreign. Demonstrations where college students protested publicly—sometimes with violence— shocked us with the antithesis to our vow of obedience. Love-ins defied

83

our vow of chastity. Viewed from inside the security of the convent walls, the outside world seemed scary with its strife, war, and assassinations. The convent served as a safe haven from the mayhem jolting the country, but I felt like a stranger in my own world.

As tie-dyed shirts and long hair ushered in the era of the hippies, we veiled our chopped hair in black as a sign of consecration. While kids my age broke free of the social constraints of their parents, we tied ourselves to the rules of religious life. Free love floated through city parks, but we vowed virginity in the sexual vacuum of the convent. Protestors invaded campus administration buildings with sit-ins, but we subjected our wills to obedience of our superiors. Hippies lauded LSD as a drug of choice, while we inhaled the incense of religion. Popular songs from the Doors, Grateful Dead, and Jefferson Airplane pounded beats of acid rock, while we chanted the peaceful psalms.

While colleges across the country boiled over with the counterculture revolution of music, drugs, political activism, and sex, we struggled with just getting to school. None of us had driven a vehicle for two years in the novitiate.

Our three Omaha-born nuns took turns driving us to the college since they knew the roads. Sister Mary Judith, who came from a large family with numerous brothers she carted to and from sports, felt right at home with the minivan's manual shift. Lacking experience in driving a stick shift, I gave thanks for someone else behind the wheel. Our days as junior professed nuns were crammed with prayer and studies to attain teaching certificates. Since all of us had the same education major, we attended the same classes together. We must have looked like a nun herd traveling together for our seminars. Whenever we passed other students, conversations stopped, and eyes darted away or gaped at our black habits.

Wherever I went, in the halls, in class, or to the cafeteria, my cheeks flushed at the quizzical gazes. Although we were the same age as the other students, and probably the same religion, and all at the university for the same education, a tremendous gap loomed between the regular college girls and us nuns. As the girls twittered about the newest fashions, we wore the same black religious habits everyday.

"These girls are my age and yet seem so immature," I mused to myself. Then, I countered my own thoughts, "But they seem so carefree and laugh so easily." Their easy-going mannerisms and youthful enthusiasm lightened the air around me. Striving to be a good nun, I suppressed my own desire for laughter in favor of maintaining religious decorum. As one class progressed, the teacher paired students up for a teamwork activity. To my dismay, I ended up partnered with a girl who had been busy planning what to wear. From the frown on her face, she didn't find the pairing any more to her liking than I did. In spite of our misgivings, we pulled our desks together to tackle the assignment.

"Hi, I'm Susan. Everyone calls me Susie," my workmate introduced herself.

Attempting to meet her gaze, I return a polite response imitating her introduction, "It's nice to meet you, Susie. I'm Sister Mary Patricia, and everybody calls me Sister Mary Patricia." We laughed together, and the atmosphere softened.

"I've never worked with a nun before," Susie confessed, looking straight into my eyes. "Do you want to teach elementary or high school?"

"Oh, I haven't given it much thought."

"You haven't!" Susie wailed in dismay. "Why not? I've always dreamt about being a kindergarten teacher. I'd like to teach at the elementary school that I attended right there on Underwood Avenue."

"It really doesn't make any difference what I want to do," I explained, looking at my desktop. "I'll teach wherever I am sent by Mother Superior."

"You don't get to choose what you will teach or where you will teach?" Susie's tone conveyed horror.

"No. I took the vow of obedience and promised that I would follow whatever Mother Superior commands. Our order has both elementary and high schools in Nebraska, Iowa, Michigan, and New York. I'll be happy no matter where I am sent," I expounded, more to reassure myself than for Susie's enlightenment.

"That's cool," Susie shrugged her shoulders as she leaned her head to one side. Then she added, "I guess."

I looked at the floor, my black veil shading my face, and repeated my vows of obedience, poverty, and chastity. "Thy will be done," I prayed to God.

After taking our vows, we also moved out of the novitiate and into the Motherhouse next door. Mother Monica no longer dictated every minute of our lives. She had accomplished her job of taking us as young teenage girls to form us into religious nuns. Now, I reported to Mother Imelda, the top authority of the American Province in our order.

One day, Mother Imelda summoned me to her office. Fidgeting with nervousness, I awaited her entrance. In the past when Mother Monica called me into her office, the conference entailed directional guidance or a behavioral correction for me, but this time I was at a loss for the purpose. Mother Imelda had the reputation of being an even-keeled leader in spite of the turbulent times of change raging within the Catholic Church, but other than informal occasions, I hadn't had much contact with our Mother Provincial, much less a personal conference in her office.

"Good morning, Sister Mary Patricia. I'm so glad that you could make it," Mother Imelda greeted me. The tall commanding nun sat down behind her cluttered desk. I uncrossed my ankles and sat up to attention.

"Your father phoned me, Sister," the Mother divulged in a serious business tone.

"What's wrong?" I interrupted, raising my hands to cover my ears to shield the incoming blow. Mother Imelda's long angular face broadened with a redeeming smile.

"Oh, everything is fine with your family. Your parents need your help." She pulled a little black coin purse from her top drawer. "It seems your grandmother in Sioux City had a stroke a few weeks ago."

I let my breath escape. Mother Imelda studied me before continuing, "Now that your parents left the Midwest, no one is able to care for your grandmother, and she must go to California. Your father asked if you could accompany her to San Diego."

I slumped back in the chair in dismay. "Escort my paralyzed grandmother from Iowa to a new convalescent home in California?" I thought. "No way."

Mother Imelda saw my rising panic. "I've arranged for you to take the bus to Sioux City tomorrow, Friday. You will have to miss one day of school, but I feel that this is more important." She wrinkled her brows beginning the details of my journey. I listened, knowing I had no choice.

"The hospital has agreed to transport you and your grandmother by ambulance to Junction Falls, about an hour away, to fly out to catch the flight to California. Your parents have purchased six airline tickets to accommodate the stretcher for your grandmother," Mother Imelda explained as if reading a prepared program. I sat stupefied, picturing my grandmother and me hogging six seats with a gurney on the airplane!

"Upon landing in San Diego, your parents will meet you with transportation for your grandmother to be driven to the facility, and you'll fly back here," the Mother Provincial finished, clearly pleased with the arrangements.

I tried to compose myself while inside the bile of panic churned. The task seemed far beyond Herculean. I yanked myself together enough to emit a faint assent. I feared doing the task alone, but duty would compel me to comply.

The Mother handed me the small black coin purse. "Your father sent a check. Here is some money you might need for cab fare or meals."

Unsnapping the closure on top of the purse, I counted the bills. Feeling unease at handling money for the first time in over two years, I recounted the two hundred dollars.

"I don't need this much, Mother," I offered half of it back, not wanting to be responsible for so much money. But she bade me keep it.

"I'll give the rest back to you when I return," I promised, lowering my head in submission. "Thank you, Mother, for the opportunity to help my family." I trained my eyes on the floor as I left to hide my naked terror.

The following morning, I boarded the Greyhound bus for Sioux City—all alone, like a nun robot on a mission. I stared straight ahead to show my dedicated focus to the task at hand. "This shouldn't be that difficult," I preached to myself. "The plans are all made and tickets purchased. All I have to do is follow orders, which I'm very good at doing." My sense of duty bolstered me. Plus, I was pleasing my Heavenly Father, my earthy father, and my religious superior—hitting the obedience trifecta.

"Good morning, Sister," friendly bus passengers startled me with kindness.

"Right over here, Sister," one woman ushered me to my seat.

"Here, let me help you with that bag," a gentleman hoisted my small black suitcase onto the rack. Some travelers even bent in half bows, smiling in recognition at a representative of God. For the first time, I stretched a little taller in my black habit.

The bus cruised up the highway for the three-hour drive. Soon snowflakes whizzed past the cold frosty windows, and wind howled over the engine noise. The snow built into a full-blown storm while anxiousness ate at me. We rolled in late to Sioux City, where I caught a taxi to the hospital.

As the cab driver pulled up to the entrance to St. Joseph's Hospital, I dug into my deep black serge pockets for the purse. Glancing in the rear mirror over his head, the driver noticed my fumbling. Embarrassment flushed my cheeks. I hoped my clumsiness didn't give my maiden journey secret away.

"Sister, don't worry about it. This one's on me. I've got kids in the Catholic school, and the nuns are always raising money for one thing or another. I've got you covered today." The driver clicked the meter to "no charge."

I clamped my mouth shut to avoid gaping at him. "Thank you for your kindness, and God bless you," I managed to convey my sincerity while exiting the taxi.

As the snowstorm unleashed more fury, I climbed the hospital steps. My nerves jangled on a higher note for our tight schedule to reach Junction Falls. We had to leave the hospital by ambulance at one o'clock to make the three o'clock plane.

Snow blew sideways outside my grandma's window, but her eyes lit up when she recognized me dressed in my full religious habit. Since she could not speak after her stroke, her eyes conveyed surprise. "What are you doing here?" she seemed to ask.

"Hi, Grandma. It's so good to see you," I grasped her hand in comfort and gave her a peck on her cheek. "I'm here to take you to California to be with Mom and Dad."

A light knocking interrupted us, and a well-manicured nurse entered. "You must be Sister Mary Patricia," she took in my habit as confirmation. "I know you're headed for Junction Falls, but I have some bad news. This snowstorm has ice-packed the highways. They're impassable. Our ambulance cannot go out until the highway patrol declares the roads safe." The apologetic look on her face belied her stern voice.

My shoulders dropped. I knew a winter storm raged outside, but could only think of our flight connection in Junction Falls. "Isn't there anything you can do?" I pleaded.

"I understand your situation, but we have to take every precaution with our patients and their safety. Why don't you go to the waiting room, and I'll come to get you as soon as I hear anything," she shuffled me out of the room, her pudgy middle age stature reeking of someone quite adept at giving orders.

I slumped on the couch in the waiting area, wracking my head for a solution. An older gentleman entered the room dressed in his hospital gown. When my eyes flinched at his face and extremities that glowed red, looking as they had been burnt to a crisp, I jumped up, embarrassed by my own reaction. I paced to the window to stare at the blowing snow instead of the man.

"I didn't mean to startle you," the man said.

"Oh, I'm sorry. I'm just a little jumpy. This snow is complicating our plans."

"Supposed to keep up all night," the stranger tossed out casually.

"Oh no, that's terrible. What am I going to do?" I lamented aloud. But inwardly, I blamed God for setting me up in this storm without any superior to tell me what to do. I had no idea how to proceed with a Plan B.

"Nothing you can do about the weather, Sister," he ran his eyes up and down me like he had never seen a nun before. I squirmed at his uninhibited gawking.

"The snow got to me too last night," he confessed, pointing to his red arms. "This here is frostbite. I had too many drinks and stumbled into a snowdrift and fell asleep."

"Oh, it looks very painful. But at least you will heal." "I'll be good as new in a few days. What about you, Sister? What are you doing?"

Despite that the two of us had nothing in common, I dropped onto the couch, pouring out my worries about my grandmother, the snowstorm, and how the lack of the ambulance would cause us to miss the flight out of Junction Falls to California. He sat with patience listening to every detail.

"I have never been in a situation like this. I don't know what to do. I might call Mother Imelda and ask her," I pondered aloud for possible solutions.

"You don't have to call her. Think for yourself," he admonished, sensing my naïveté. His words "think for yourself" slapped me. I perused the alcoholic speaker of the words, floored by the irony of the source.

"Since the highways are impassable, don't use them. Hire a private plane and fly to Junction Falls. You will get off the roads and save time," he contended, picking up the Yellow Pages on the end table beneath the phone.

"Thanks for your help, but I could never do anything like that," I resorted to the Custody of the Eyes for safety.

"It's your only hope," I heard him urge as I glanced at the clock ticking away on the wall and then to the window to note any change in weather. The snow blew sideways.

"I'll call and arrange it for you," he offered. "All we have to do is to get you and your grandma to the local private airport, just about a mile from here. No highways. You'll be there in a minute." The details of the plan seemed to come so easy to him.

From his use of the word "we," I felt like we were now a team on a mission.

I acquiesced with a nod. He dialed one of the numbers. I closed my eyes, hoping for a miracle to transport me back to the safety of the convent. I had no idea how much a private plane would cost, but I guessed it would be more than my two hundred dollars. I clutched my little black coin purse in despair, while my face no doubt revealed my thoughts.

"Don't worry about the cost, Sister. These pilots are friends of mine, and they can bill your convent or your father."

"You make it sound like your plan could work," I clutched at his slim sliver of hope to make our flight to California.

"Of course, it's going to work," he pronounced as if he made arrangements like these every day. "Now, get that nurse to ready your grandmother and tell her to have the hospital ambulance take you to Rocky Point private airfield. Time's a wasting."

Having been trained so well in obedience, I jumped up and located the nurse to make the necessary arrangements. "Are you there, God? You're not going to believe this one!" I uttered a prayer of thanks as we readied my grandmother for transport.

In the tumult of the blizzard, the ambulance drove slowly through the deserted city streets to the outskirts of town. The reflection from the runway lights cast the only light into the darkness of whirling snow. The tiny airplane seemed to cower against the storm. With care, the ambulance drivers and the two pilots drug my grandmother's limp body over the wing and into the back seat of the small four-passenger airplane.

As I climbed into the seat next to Grandma, I took her hand and wiped the tears from her eyes as the plane took off. "I hope and pray that everything will work out, Grandma," I implored, as much for myself as for her.

My breath bounced out of me as the tiny aircraft made its way through the turbulence unseen in the darkness. Terror ran through my veins as flashes of lightening bolted outside the window. "What am I doing, for God's sake?" I rebuffed myself, feeling queasy and squeezing my grandmother's hand for comfort.

Flying in a Midwest blizzard at night with two strange men and my paralyzed crying grandmother seemed surreal, but my worry that we would miss the flight to San Diego kept my nerves frittering on the edge. Each radio squawk updating the pilots on our California flight's status flicked me raw.

I fretted the possibilities: If we missed the flight, what would I do?

Where would I take Grandma? I raised my eyebrows to heaven, "Where are you, God? I really need you now." I prayed like I had never prayed before.

As we dropped into our descent into Junction Falls, red lights on the instrument panel flashed. "Why did those lights on your dashboard go red?" I shot at the two pilots.

"That means we are on instrument landing, Sister," the co-pilot answered without turning around. "We have no visibility. We'll be just fine. Don't worry." His calm voice conveyed the pattern of routine, that instrument flying was normal.

I split my attention between listening to the tower commands and trying to comfort my grandmother as the pilots steadied the plane for landing. "Thanks be to God," I exhaled as we touched down and came to a safe stop on the runway. The pilots taxied the plane over to the side of the runway, announcing the good news that our incoming flight to California hadn't arrive yet due to the weather. My hunched tight shoulders dropped back into place, knowing we would make our plane.

After an interminable wait in the small plane with Grandma wailing, the bright lights of the big arriving plane heralded the next leg of the journey. With profuse thanks, I took the bill for the charter flight explaining that the funds would be sent within a week. The pilots trusted my habit for payment.

After an airport ambulance transferred Grandma to the awaiting 737 to San Diego, I followed the portable bed that the attendants carried into the plane, trying to calm my grandmother with soft reassuring words. "Don't worry, we'll be with Mom and Dad real soon," I whispered, talking to both of us.

All eyes on board focused on us, as our parade inched down the aisle to our prepared special block of three rows of two seats each on one side of the plane. Using three seats next to the window, the airline had placed a stretcher on top of the seatbacks for Grandmother to lie on, surrounded on all three sides by a privacy curtain. My seat remained outside of the curtain next to the aisle.

The flight attendants prepared for take off by strapping Grandmother to the stretcher as I tried to ignore her soft sobbing sounds. Buckling my seatbelt, I sank back into the cushion and tried to compose my mind and shed the tenseness clinging heavy on me like my habit. The past ten hours of anxiousness had frayed me into exhaustion. I inhaled the airplane food, having failed to eat all day. With my eyes closed, I leaned my head back against the headrest but my veil headdress prevented me from further comfort.

At midnight, our flight landed in San Diego. The flashing red lights of the ambulance making its way to our airplane seemed commonplace now. The other passengers waited in their seats as the flight crew and ambulance staff moved my grandmother on her stretcher into the ambulance bound for her new nursing home.

I spent most of the short weekend with my family reliving the story about Grandma, the flights, and the helpful people along the way. At first, I felt a little conspicuous wearing my religious habit at home instead of my old street clothes, but soon I relaxed into the role of the nun. The habit was part of me, and it had worked magic on the trip.

"You can throw all my old clothes out now, Mom. I'll be wearing my nun's habit from now on," I announced, feeling a sense of pride in my black religious garb.

"God does work in mysterious ways," I mused on the return flight back to the convent. I closed my eyes, pleased at the successful completion of my first mission as a nun on my own in the outside world.

Arriving back in Omaha, I sought out Mother Imelda to report back and return the money.

"How was your trip, Sister?" the Mother inquired with questioning eyebrows.

"Went just like clockwork," I fibbed, handing her the small black coin purse still containing the two hundred dollars. "This was my first adventure in the world on my own, and I think I perceived the power of the habit."

She winked at me. Her knowing smile said that I had come of age experiencing the impact of the religious habit.

Chapter 10

Modifying the Habit

Life in the convent puttered along the same, day in, day out, until one day the following year. The auditorium at the Motherhouse twittered with unparalleled excitement. All of the nuns in our order within the two-hour drive assembled for an unheard of convocation in direct response to the edicts of Vatican II. While I was in high school, Pope John XXIII had summoned the Vatican II council to overhaul antiquated elements within the Catholic Church. The council deliberated for three years, finishing in 1965, the year I entered the convent. Another three years passed before many of the changes wrought by the council finally filtered into the sacred walls of our Omaha convent.

The worldwide spirit urging the Catholic Church to reach out to the contemporary world brought about Vatican II. With bishops hailing from around the world, Catholic leaders came together in the spirit of "Aggiornamento," or renewal. The conclave of bishops labored to delineate a path of revival, like opening a window of fresh air to initiate an extraordinary transformation of the Catholic Church. Sixteen documents, written by the council and approved by the Pope, updated all facets of faith from ecumenism to the role of the laity. Two particular documents—one on the sacred liturgy and the second on the renewal of religious life—painted broad reaching effects into our everyday lives as nuns.

Sweeping changes in the sacred liturgy turned the altar away from the wall to face the people and authorized the use of vernacular languages in worship to replace the Latin Mass. For nuns, the document urging religious life to adapt to the modern world eliminated outdated rites and customs—all for our mission to connect with our communities. After we had returned to our baptismal names, rumors circulated that modifying the habit would soon follow.

Mother Imelda walked up to the podium, commanding attention without a spoken word. An abrupt silence fell across the room.

"My dear sisters. Since Vatican II, we have expended energy trying to return to the spirit of our founders. In the 1800s, our founders adapted the dress of the poor peasant working class women, and that habit has been handed down through the decades, never changing," Mother Imelda began, reciting the history of the habit with her business monotone voice. She noted that wearing a veil in keeping with modesty and keeping seculars at a safe distance cloistered us from the world as much as protected us.

"In the spirit of renewal, we have been directed to discard our traditional habits to return to the original intent of representing the poor working class of OUR day," Mother Imelda peered over her reading glasses to size up the anxious faces. The flock of black-draped nuns sat at attention listening to their fate as prescribed by the council. Most of the younger nuns nodded their heads in agreement while the older sisters sitting in the front left section looked at each other with consternation.

"I appointed a commission of sisters last year to design a modified habit, and we're here today to see their work," Mother Imelda announced with her eyes darting around the room to assess the number of threatened nuns. "In the spirit of sisterhood and renewal, I give you your habit of the future. This is a first baby step in a total modernization of religious wear."

Mother Imelda stepped aside, and Sister Mary Christine, one of my high school math teachers, walked onto the stage in the new contemporary dress. A modified short veil sat back on her head like a headband from ear to ear exposing her beautiful auburn bangs. A simple mid-calf black skirt revealing black sheer stockings had replaced the long black tunic. Gone were the ugly black nun shoes—in their place, a pair of plain black Mary Jane type shoes. A modest black three-quarter length sleeved blouse, buttoning in the back, set off by a white Peter-Pan collar replaced the neck-pinching wimple. At first glance, the new modified habit reminded me of the attire similar to that of a postulant. But the sheer stockings and modern shoes updated the new habit…nothing to be premiered on the cover of Vogue, but a noticeable increment in the right direction.

Gasps swept the hall as nuns strained to inventory what they would soon be wearing. Snorts and gulps revealed the horror of some while others nodded approval.

Sister Mary Christine stood on stage as the spectacle for all to ogle. She blushed realizing how exposed she felt to each staring eye. My heart felt for her as the object of everyone's attention. Fingers pointed, and whispers rumbled. Discarding religious decorum, the nuns reacted on impulse to their new modified habit.

But the new habit didn't strike me as much as the color surrounding Sister Mary Christine's face. I couldn't help myself from uttering, "Red hair! Who would have thought that she had red hair?" I poked Sister Mary Eileen. "During all those math classes, I sat right in front of her and never knew she was a redhead."

The sight of the red hair tossed me into reflection. As my high school teacher, her name had been Sister Mary Thomas. I had no inkling what her real name was or what she looked like hidden from view by the habit. I felt so stupid assuming that she had been a nameless, non-person nun, yet as I glanced down at my black tunic and scapular, the same depersonalizing attire hid the real me from view.

"Thank you for modeling our new modified habit, Sister," Mother Imelda closed the visual inspection. "It takes a lot of courage to be the first," the Mother voiced her sentiments with a nod toward Sister Mary Christine, who turned to leave the stage.

Mother Imelda faced the sea of black habits once more. "I know that this change will be received by all of you in good faith. The timing of your adapting the new habit is up to each of you individually. Most will embrace this quickly with open hearts and minds. Others of you may take some time of adjustment." Her eyes zeroed in on the faces of the older nuns who had lived in the same religious habit for decades.

Most of the nuns—including me—opted to dress in the new modified habit as soon as possible, glad to be rid of cumbersome folds of fabric and headpieces. Taking off the tunic, scapular, wimple, veil, and rosary for the last time, I shed the heavy clothes like a snake climbing out of his own skin. Folding them up for the last time, I thought of the respect these holy clothes carried. When taking my grandmother to San Diego, my fellow bus passengers, the cab driver, the alcoholic frostbit man, and the pilots bowed in respect of the habit. The black garb garnered automatic prestige. I would miss that.

I looked at the pile of black material. The odd prudish habit had also been a divisive wedge in pursuing personal relationships. We appeared as nonsexual beings, void of individual personalities, floating, legless robots. The change of habit would be more than just a change of outfit; it would be a true coming out.

A personal journey led to receiving the habit, and now changing to the newer one would also be a personal journey. The real Patty had taken on the identity of Sister Mary Patricia, habit and all—assuming the decorum, speech, and persona of the nun. But I wondered what I would be like in the new attire. My face would be visible in front of everyone without a veil for hiding. Would I be vain again with my brown bangs showing?

The next week after Easter break, we returned to college ready to finish up most of our education classes to prepare to teach next year in one of our mission schools. We looked different than we had a week earlier marching out to the van. Feeling like a kindergartener on the first day of school, I declared to the other nuns in the van as I slid behind the steering wheel, "I feel about thirty pounds lighter."

"I didn't think that I could make this adjustment so quickly, but this lighter veil feels like a feather compared to what we had before," Sister Mary Judith voiced what we all felt. Heads nodded in agreement.

"I can't believe how I can see to the side without moving my whole body," Sister Mary Barbara added, rocking her head from side to side like a windshield wiper.

Sister Mary Judith rambled on about how relieved she was to not wear the clunky industrial nun shoes, compared to the new Mary Janes. Sister Mary Barbara shared her fashion tips for styling her now seen bangs. Sporting our new modified habits, we chatted en route to the campus, looking almost like normal co-eds.

Near the college, I paused on a steep hill waiting for the red light to turn green. When the light turned, I clutched into first gear, but to my dismay, the van rolled backwards picking up speed down the hill.

"Shit," I yelled, stomping on the brake to stop. Sister Mary Judith paused mid sentence, and two gasps flew from the back of the van. Then silence. Surprised at my use of profanity, I shot my eyes to the rear view mirror.

"I am so sorry for that outburst," I gushed an apology for my outlandish break from religious decorum. "I don't know where that came from." I looked down at the steering wheel, but inwardly giggled at my inane gut response to panic.

"Sister Mary Patricia, you take off the old veil and the old self comes back," a voice from the back chided. "I haven't heard that word in ages. It used to be one of my favorites."

Her words echoed in me: "Take off the old veil and the old self comes back." I wondered what other parts of my old self would reappear.

Custody of the Eyes proved to be a safe retreat as I walked down the familiar corridor of the college, feeling the stinging stares of the astonished students doing double takes at the new habits. Some even lobbed, "Looking good, Sister." I stared at the linoleum hall floor.

As I entered my reading methods class, Susie aimed a pensive glare at me. Sliding into the seat next to her, I half smiled, waiting for her reaction.

"Sister Mary Patricia, is that really you? I barely recognized you. You look so different." She arched her eyebrows.

"Same old me, just a change of habit," I reassured her. Like a schoolgirl sporting a new outfit—wanting reassurance, but not wanting to be the center of attention—I giggled with my new secular friend.

"You look so young and innocent," Susie tried to hide the surprise in her voice. A wide grin broadened across her face as she confessed, "I thought you were much older, but you look about my age now."

Her words made me look comparatively at her hair, makeup, and dress. She appeared very pretty. Her artful application of makeup gave her an older, sophisticated aura. In juxtaposition, I recalled my plain face earlier that day in the mirror. I had tried to comb my short wispy flat straight bangs into style, but Buster Brown or maybe Moe of the Three Stooges looked back at me from the mirror.

"You're right, Susie," I finally answered her, feeling naked and plain. "You do look older and more mature than I do now without the full habit on. I can't hide behind the habit any more."

"Oh, Sister, I didn't mean it that way. You look great," Susie rushed to make me feel better. "But I have some extra makeup, if you ever want to borrow it, Sister."

"Maybe a little blush some day, Susie," I tossed back, thinking about my daily use of the mirror now.

As we adjusted to our new habits, the feeling of hopeful change swept through the Catholic world. But the change collided with one immovable force. Pope Paul VI wrote the Humanae Vitae, banning the practice of artificial birth control. This papal decision decreed during the summer 1968 seemed to be a giant step backward from the new spirit put forth by Vatican II. One swipe of the pen dashed the hopes that the church would listen to the pleas of over burdened married couples and the advice of medical doctors to sanction use of the contraception pill.

We had learned in school that the purpose of marriage was to have children. "Be fruitful and multiply," the Bible said. The Church taught that any artificial means of preventing conception acted as an intrusion in God's deigned plan. Abstaining from sex was the only church-approved method of birth control. My family, among many other obedient Catholic families, struggled with this predicament; Mom and Dad lived up to their responsibility as good parents, churning out baby after baby. When I heard the news that he signed the decree, a pain welled in me for my family. I remembered when I was in eighth grade, my Dad gathering our family of three girls for a big announcement.

"Your Mom is pregnant," he boasted.

"When is Mom due? How does she feel? Do you think it could be a boy?"

We all three chirped at once sounding like clucking hens.

But despite the surprise of Mom's pregnancy, glee shone in our eyes. "This time we'll have a boy for sure," I pronounced, knowing how much Dad longed for a son and the impossibility of Mom having four girls in a row.

Mom's biological clock ticked. Near forty years old, she felt the pressure mount, although she said nothing. We prayed for the long-awaited boy.

Five months later, Dad slipped into my bedroom at night, startling me with an announcement that he needed to take Mom to the hospital. I protested that she wasn't due yet, but fell back to sleep.

The next morning I jumped out of bed to run into my parents' bedroom. Scaring my sleeping Father, I shouted in excitement, "Did we have a boy or a girl?"

Groggy, Dad rolled over and pulled the pillow to prop himself up. He nodded, acknowledging my question, but I spotted exhaustion in his eyes.

"We had a girl. And then we had another girl!"

"What?" My shoulders drooped, and my eyes widened. "We had two girls?" I sympathized with his disappointment at five daughters.

Dad paused to search for just the right words. "They aren't right. There's something wrong with them." He wiped his eyes. "They were six weeks premature and their lungs aren't fully developed. They probably won't make it."

My heart squeezed with fright. The twins died two days later. My Mom never did see them. She just couldn't bear it. Dad, Penny, Polly, and I buried our sisters in their delicate blue and pink nightgowns. They looked like hand painted porcelain baby dolls.

Mom and Dad rarely ever spoke about the twins. But one night passing to my room in the hallway, I overheard them talking.

"There must have been some medical problem," Dad mollified mom.

Then, his voice quivered. "If the stakes had become more serious, the doctor could only save one life—yours or the babies. I know the teaching of the Catholic Church is to save the baby and let the mother go." His voice rose to shaking, "But I'm not about to let you go when you have other children that need you."

I recoiled. My hand shot to cover my mouth at the thought of the church letting my Mom die for the baby.

After the loss of the twins, my parents consulted our parish pastor about the use of the emerging birth control pill. I hoped that Mom would be able to take the new pill because of her unusual circumstances—her age and having just lost twins.

Our parish priest listened to Mom and Dad's request, but he refused to allow my mother to use birth control since it was against Catholic teachings. My parents returned home, their sagging heads and worried expressions conveying the pastor's verdict. Despite feeling spurned by the church that they loved, they set aside their disappointment to heed the command of the priest. Mom continued as the compliant baby-making factory while the question of the church's attitude toward birth control festered inside me.

Three years later, Kristin was born, followed two years later by Robbie. Whenever Dad convened the family together, we girls, held our collective breaths praying, "Not again, not another baby."

At dinner one night in the Motherhouse, I first heard the news that the church reiterated its anti-birth control stance. The pros and cons of the decision bantered across the table much like the discussion of the other changes the church had initiated. Unlike the other nuns, my stomach twisted thinking what my parents went through with the loss of the twins and then having to face the unknown consequences with deliveries of two more children when Mom had long passed healthy child bearing age. Many friends in our parish struggled to support large families—some with eight or ten children.

I had hoped that sanctioned birth control would come in the sweeping renewal to bring relief to over burdened families. But the church seemed to turn a deaf ear to the earthly needs of people. The decree forced loyal Catholics to face the tough decision of remaining faithful or defying the church to limit the size of their families.

The church's decision to oppose contraception grated on me. The birth control issue replayed in my head like a horrible movie rerun. My mind repeated my parents' bedroom debates about practicing the pre-scribed religious dictates or following their hearts. My parents believed that their beloved church would guide them through the hardships of childbearing, but it failed to meet their needs. While supposedly studying, my attention festered with anger at the unmarried bishops who made the church laws and how the church could rule on what goes on in the privacy of the bedroom.

I kept my disappointment with the church's decision on birth control to myself, knowing how to play my part. But the seed of dissatisfaction had sprouted. Outwardly I supported the rulings of the church, but inwardly doubt ate at the church's credibility.

Months of college classes flew by as we adapted to the changing church hoping for meaningful transformation. During the metamorphosis, my father called upon me via the Mother Provincial to aid him again in the summer. This time, to accompany my other grandparents on their first flight to California. I agreed to fly with my seventy-year-old grandparents from South Dakota to San Diego to visit my family. They had never been to California before, nor had they ever been on a plane.

I met my grandparents in South Dakota to fly to Los Angeles where the three of us sat in the terminal waiting for our connecting flight to San Diego. People stared at the questionable threesome—two odd looking seniors and a nun. I had grown used to peculiar glances outside the convent. Because my grandparents hadn't traveled outside South Dakota, they ogled people, taking in the oddities that comprise a cosmopolitan city, when a Japanese businessman walked by.

"Goddam Jap," my grandfather yelled, jumping out of his seat. His face scowling with contempt, he waggled his finger in the Japanese man's face. "You killed my son!"

I tried to restrain Grandpa, his fiery face and flailing arms attracting the attention of people who scurried to avoid the confrontation. I pulled at Grandpa's coat to drag him back to his seat, my stomach clenching at his outburst. I had never seen my grandfather upset. My grandmother sat paralyzed in horror, staring at the Japanese businessman.

"This isn't the man that killed your son. That was a long time ago," I eased my grandfather back into his seat and stroked his arm, hoping that his anger would subside.

When he quieted, I hurried over to the Japanese gentleman to make amends. "I'm so sorry. He didn't mean any harm," I wailed in a penitential voice looking straight into the man's eyes to reach his heart. I stood tall in my modified habit ready to defend my grandfather, but trembled inside. "That is my grandfather. He lost his oldest son in the war and has never forgiven your country. You are the first Japanese he has seen, so he took his anger out on you. I'm so sorry." My eyes pleaded with the man for forgiveness.

"You should be sorry," the man rebuked me, shooting daggers with his eyes. "With anger like that in your family, you shouldn't be representing the church." The man huffed once, scoffed, and spun off on his way.

The crowd cleared as I returned to my grandparents. "He's gone now, Grandpa. Everything will be fine," I soothed him, patting his knee in reassurance. Grandma and Grandpa grasped each other's hands in support.

Sitting in the airport terminal, I battled shame. I didn't know whom to blame—Grandpa, the Japanese man, or myself. Even with the modified habit, I represented the church. That meant upholding the church's values.

Room for dissension within the ranks within the church did not exist; I had to face my disagreement with the rule that banned using artificial birth control. For the first time, I felt like an outsider dressed in religious habit, representing the church and all it stood for, but unable to agree with its rulings. I consented with the church up to now, but couldn't fake the horror of supporting what I didn't agree with. As in the habit, no gray existed in the church. Only black and white.

Chapter 11

Igniting Things Buried Deep

The heavy air of anticipation weighed on me as I waited for Mother Imelda to share my future teaching assignment. After our junior year of college, the convent deemed us ready to teach school. We would finish up studies for our diplomas during the summer. Beads of perspiration ran down my cheek on that hot humid August afternoon in her office, the heat making me glad that I no longer wore the warm heavy veil of last year. One thing for certain: Mother Imelda made the choice about my future without any input from me. I was assigned; I had to go. I awaited my mission, my duty. I owed that obedience to God.

"Sister Mary Patricia," the Mother began, sitting forward in her chair ready to dispense the direction of my life. "I need your help next year. I'm assigning you to one of our smaller missions in Iowa."

The Mother, reading the blank look on my face, painted the location for me. "Our order has staffed Salix, a rural community right outside Sioux City, for many years. As a matter of fact," the Mother confided, hoping to elicit my confidence, "the four nuns presently assigned there have been working longer than they should have, becoming overly tied to the people and their staunch ways." She paused to see if I understood before daubing my future with broad strokes of color.

"The parishioners are very devout Catholics, proud of their church and school, but the new era of change in the church as not been well accepted in Salix," she divulged. I squinted at Mother Imelda, wondering why she would send me, a young first year teacher, into that position fraught with potential antagonism.

"The present staff of nuns has chosen to remain in the traditional habit only reinforcing resistance to the renewal movement. I'm swapping out three of the four nuns that have been there, hoping your new faces will bring in the fresh air of the Holy Spirit," Mother Imelda put the final dabs on her painting of my assignment. The small quaint convent of four nuns sounded blissful—almost like a real home, but the atmosphere of the parish cried out anything but Eden.

"Now, about your teaching assignment," she motored right on, without waiting for a response from me. "The elementary school consists of grades one through eight, with four combination classrooms. You will be teaching grades three and four. Sister Mary Sylvia will be the school's principal and your superior in the convent." I smiled at the mention of Sister Mary Sylvia, who broke into laughter with ease—the opposite of Mother Monica in the novitiate.

Mother Imelda's agenda was clear—to send a cadre of younger nuns donning modified habits to transform the people mired in older traditions of the parish. I sat up a little straighter recognizing her confidence in me.

The four of us assigned nuns drove into Salix. The elementary school, convent, and church with three contrasting types of architecture stood side-by-side, but together the dominant center of the life in the tiny blink-and-you'll-miss-it town. In the middle of the church's property, a big white Mid-western two-story farmhouse served as the school, set back from the street curb across a lawn.

Flanking one side of the school, a newer brick ranch home functioned as the convent while the traditional gothic-looking church loomed on the opposite side. I pondered the three buildings in a row, like a religious stripe across the fields of Iowa, so different from the industrial appearing Omaha schools. "Who knows," I thought, "I might even find God in the cornfields in Iowa."

After carrying our bags and books into the convent, Sister Mary Sylvia's cheery voice rang out: "We need to get ourselves organized!"

She directed the four of us to cluster around the small circular table in the convent dining room. I wondered exactly what we had to organize. I had never participated in an organizational meeting. My life had been formulated for me; I just followed orders.

One by one, the nuns spoke up, volunteering for household responsibilities like cleaning and doing the laundry. I committed to sweeping and mopping the floors three days per week, signing up for familiar tasks from the novitiate.

"Let's look at the days of cooking," Sister Mary Sylvia moved on to the next item on her list. The other three nuns promptly offered their culinary skills for certain days.

"Which days do you want?" Sister Mary Agnes demanded, peering into my face with her eyes protruding behind dirty bifocal glasses. In her seventies and the most senior of us, she glared at me, her faced framed with gray wiry hair.

I sat mute, resorting to the protection of the Custody of the Eyes. I had no skills with meal planning or cooking.

"Well, what's wrong with you, anyway?" she badgered, leaning in closer to give her words more power.

"I don't cook. As a novice, I helped in the vegetable pit, but I've never cooked," I sputtered, feeling once again like I sat back in Sister Mary Cleopha's high school algebra class. My face flushed with automatic embarrassment.

"I can set the table and do the dishes," I offered to mollify the nun.

"Can you read?" Sister Mary Agnes blared.

"Yes, I can read," I doused my voice with forced calm, praying she would drop it.

"If you can read then you can cook," Sister Mary Agnes proclaimed, settling back into her chair crossing her arms in triumph. Case closed.

All eyes at the table riveted on my reaction. Fixing my gaze over at the old nun, I agreed to cook, taking on my two days of preparing meals…just like Dora Dumbhead in high school volunteering to be boiled in oil for Sister Mary Cleopha.

I threw myself into learning to cook and teaching third and fourth graders. Life in Salix sailed along into the first parent-teacher conferences.

Wanting to look organized, like I knew what I was doing, I straightened my desk and my clothing. I wanted to convey competency to avoid appearing like a rookie first year teacher. I rummaged though the file of papers to ensure that all the work samples were ready for Mr. and Mrs. Brooks' third grade son, Ben.

"Hi, Sister," a strong male baritone voice greeted me. "I'm sorry I'm a little late, but I had a scheduling problem."

I looked up from my paperwork, my sight colliding with a set of bright twinkling warm brown eyes. A broad, boyish grin crept over Mr. Brooks' face as he sauntered into the classroom and sat down at ease in the chair closest to my desk. I squirmed in my chair.

"I'm glad you could make it. Will Mrs. Brooks be joining us?" I asked, looking at the door in hope of female companionship. "No, she won't be able to make it today. I apologize for her absence, so you'll just have to put up with me," Mr. Brooks let a playful smile dance on his face.

"Oh, that's fine," I reassured Mr. Brooks, fidgeting through the pile of papers. Rarely did fathers attend parent conferences alone; I fumbled around for words. "We'll just go through some of Ben's work and discuss how we can work together. You can share our talk with your wife, and if she needs to talk with me, I can meet with her later."

I regretted the close proximity of the chair that I had positioned right next to mine so both teacher and parent could view student work. I hadn't been that physically close to a man for such a long time. "Was that Jade East he was wearing?" I wondered as my nose detected a scent I remembered from high school days. The aroma of his aftershave brought back memories of my high school boyfriend.

Mike maneuvered the Chevy just around the corner of the streetlight, parking down a secluded road with the sole light casting a dim glimmer that couldn't reach the back seat. Soft moonlight filtered through the window as he slid over near me, and we once again fell into our making out routine. I looked up at the steamy windows as our passion escalated. Every ounce of me turned to putty as Mike wrapped his arms around me. Most junior boys I knew couldn't grow peach fuzz facial hair, but his testosterone-infused beard stubble scratched my soft face when he kissed me. Jade East, the cologne he wore, rubbed off on me. Later in the night, the essence transferred to my pillow, reinforcing dreams of being loved. Like a sexual drug, his hot and sensual Italian composure, screaming "machismo," sparked vulnerability in me. My body wanted more.

Sweeping his hand with a light touch across the nape of my neck, my heart quickened. His left hand cradled my chin and pulled my face to his. I was sure Mike could hear the pounding of my heart that thumped in my ears. He pushed his body tight against mine as my pulse throbbed against his chest. I arched my back in his arms.

His kiss was ever so innocent in the beginning. But as his ardor grew, his kisses raged. Mike's tongue searched for my mine, circling, sucking—shooting outward waves of pleasure through my tingling breasts. His breath blew like a hot wind, zinging goose bumps down by neck. I pushed against him harder and cuddled in his embrace.

The voices of the nuns at school echoed through the swirling euphoria: "You must be very careful about turning a boy on. Boys will say and do anything to have their way. You could lose your virginity and go to hell." I coached myself to stay away from both sex and hell. But a few more kisses wouldn't hurt.

We dove into frenetic kissing. Mike, cresting a wave of passion, seemed to be verging out of control. I panted near breathlessness. His fervor frightened me; so did my own twirling on the brink of self-control. I backed off, stiffening to break his strong hold.

"I have to stop, Mike."

"Why? Don't tell me that you don't like this."

"Stop. Stop," I begged. But my words muffled into another kiss. He drew me in ever closer. I resisted, but he won the battle.

Pressed against his body, I felt the bulge in his pants. Panic shot through me, and I squirmed. He continued to push harder.

"Stop! Please, stop. I can't do this." My chest heaved in ragged breaths. I twisted to remove myself from his vice grip.

"Come on, baby, you know you like it. Why do you keep pushing me away?" His voice dripped into coaxing as he fumbled to keep his arms around me.

"I want to be a nun. That's why," I blurted.

"Are you alright, Sister?" Mr. Brooks reined me back to the conference. I tried to regain my composure by searching through papers. He stared at me as if he looked right into my thirsting heart, awakening to a long-buried yearning.

"I'm fine, thank you," I shot back, fighting to regroup. "Just had a long day."

"It must be a pain putting up with all of us nagging parents, explaining things over and over again numerous times," Mr. Brooks excused my lapse as tiredness.

Relaxing a bit, I confided, "This is my first year teaching, so I'm a bit nervous." I peeked up from my stack of math papers only to meet kind eyes.

"Don't worry about that. It's everyone's first year sometime at something," he encouraged, patting my hand that sat like a paperweight on the desk. I jumped at the touch of his skin on my hand.

"I like the new habits. I can see you are young and pretty, if you don't mind my saying so," Mr. Brooks sallied on. "We could never tell with the other nuns and the old habits they wore." His eyes ignited a flame extinguished long ago in me.

His sympathy coupled with his "pretty" compliment unnerved me, and his demeanor threw me off my professional, religious balance. My face reddened while my heart pounded like a drum.

I sped him through his son's schoolwork and heaved a sigh of relief as he stood to leave. He took my hand in his, offering his help. His big rough-skinned hand enclosing my small soft fingers burned.

Jade East drifted with me through the evening. I tried to push the touch of Mr. Brooks' hand and his smile from my mind, but his scent lingered. I felt like I had been hurled out into the thundering ocean, a flaming ship bouncing around without an anchor. That night, I tossed in my bed seeking a comfortable position. His touch had resurrected the primal need to be held.

"Are you there, God? It's me again, Patty," I prayed in the dark. "Is the vow of chastity supposed feel like this?"

With no further encounters with Mr. Brooks, we headed back to the Motherhouse in June where I would finish courses for my teaching credential during summer term. For the first time since entering the convent, I had feasted on independence in Salix—blossoming in being an adept teacher, learning to cook, teaching myself guitar, helping the parish with reform, and enjoying the small family-like convent.

But living the vow of chastity blindsided me, my urgings of the flesh threatening to derail my desire to serve. My stomach felt the tug-of-war as my mind yo-yoed between pleasure at my accomplishments as a nun and thoughts of Mr. Brooks. A nagging hole inside me begged for human contact.

What should have been a joyful summer looking forward to renewing my vows in August seemed more of a struggle. I had managed to quiet my feelings of isolation and replace my need for a family with the small convent in Iowa. But the larger picture loomed with a dark chasm of loneliness, while I represented a church that irked me with its backward stance on birth control in a time of renewal.

Despite the familial feel of the small religious community of four sisters in Salix and Sister Mary Sylvia's carefree openness, I continued in the strict religious practice learned in the novitiate. A cloud of asocial training suffocated every convent with its mantra of nothing personal, community first. As such, even with only four of us in the convent, we never discussed any personal feelings with anyone. No one.

My struggle with loneliness festered like an open wound. Every thought of wanting love descended into guilt. Nuns weren't supposed to want love, and with every pang of loneliness, guilt grew. To survive in the mire of guilt, I withdrew into obedience, appearing quiet and introverted. As long as I did what was required of me, I could continue to strive to be a good nun and do God's will.

But the music inside myself rocked to a discordant rhythm. My heart begged to leave the convent to seek companionship, but my brain locked in status quo yelled to stay. Not trusting that personal inner guidance system, my gut feeling, I froze with indecision. I longed to pour out pent up feelings to someone who would understand. Knowing that a priest of God would point me in the correct direction, I made an appointment to visit with Father Payne, our Motherhouse chaplain who said daily Mass during my summer back in Omaha.

With my sweaty clutched hand, I tapped lightly on the door of the Father's apartment. As Father Payne pulled the door open, I noticed that he had a few more gray hairs than last year, but still had that warm grin from ear to ear. He ushered me in, sat me down, and settled his tall slim frame in an adjacent chair.

"You look like you survived your first year out in the field," he broke the ice. "How was it?"

"Oh, Father, it's so different out there than living in the convent," I confessed.

The Father's grin returned accompanied by understanding. He rubbed his red watery allergic eyes. "Yes, you've been secluded for a few years for your religious training, but now you know what it is really like to live the three vows and serve the people," he said, studying my composure.

Taking a deep breath, I mumbled that living the three vows and serving the people wasn't all that easy. Then, I bit my lip, afraid to put my doubtful thoughts into spoken words. I didn't know how to proceed to tell him my concerns, but decided I'd just better say whatever I could.

"I don't know if I like living the vows in religious life," I blurted. "The nuns who taught me in school seemed so happy. But I have not found that happiness, only doubts and sadness about my vocation.

Everything seems black and white, good or bad, and I want to make the right decision." Immediately, I felt the pressure release from my upper back and neck, relieved that my secret had been revealed.

"What exactly are you sad about, Sister?" The Father probed, leaning forward as if to get a better angle to observe me. He seemed sincerely interested in what I had to say. I felt safe divulging my deep dark secret of doubt and lonesomeness.

"Father, I'm so lonely," I choked out the words, fighting back a rising flood of emotion. "I miss my family." The tears now tumbled out of my eyes, uncontrollably. The Father handed me a tissue from the box on a side table giving me a slight nod of approval. My chest heaved, and I struggled to get my breath. He sat quietly letting me acknowledge the turmoil within.

"I also struggle with living the vow of chastity," I spouted, biting my lip in embarrassment and averting his gaze. "But I don't want to turn my back on God just so I can satisfy my own desires. That seems so selfish. I need to make a good decision."

The Father let me argue with myself, allowing me to talk in circles, never coming to a definite decision about staying or leaving the convent. I rambled, putting to words things I hadn't been able to say to anyone; he listened.

After hearing my pros and cons of staying in the convent, he spoke, looking at me square in the eyes: "Don't worry about making a good decision, just make a decision, good."

I repeated the words to help them sink in.

"Don't worry," Father Payne reiterated.

Fret had consumed me since I walked into the convent. Anxiety held my hand, with a constant worry to please Mother Monica, Mother Imelda, and God. But I'd never experienced that day-in and day-out peace that I'd expected to find.

Father Payne had just removed the rightness and wrongness out of making a decision. He made is sound so easy. All he wanted me to do was to make a decision and then work to make it good.

Exiting his apartment, I felt so lightheaded that I almost sang down the quiet corridors of the convent. Worry seemed to flit away like a dust mote spiraling out of sight. All I had to do was to make a decision…. good!

But even with Father Payne's advice, I worried about my Heavenly Father. Would God be angry with me for quitting the nunnery after He had called me to it? As I flew to California for my annual June trip home, I still couldn't answer the question.

In the reforms of the Vatican II church renewal, our order chose to step further away from the traditional habits, dispensing with the newer modified ones after less than two years. For the first time, we would not be given our clothing; each sister had to find her own. On my annual trip home, I planned to convert from the modified habit to simple, plain street clothes.

I enlisted Mom and Penny to help outfit me in my new street clothes habit. Five years had passed since we "girls" had gone on a shopping spree.

"Look at this cool skirt," Penny held up the latest mini skirt in the store. "Try it on. You need color."

"Penny, I can't wear anything like that. It's way too short and too loud. Remember, I'm a nun," I reprimanded her, reaching instead for a dark brown mid-calf stitched down pleated skirt.

"Yuck," Penny shot out. "Looks just like a nun!" "Here's a nice suit, Pat," my mother hurried across the aisle to show me her find.

"That's beautiful, Mom," I acquiesced to her attempt. "But I think that is a bit too nice for nuns who are to be dressed as poor working class."

We rummaged through racks of clothing until we settled on a few basic skirts, blouses, and dresses. When we filed into the living room with bags of clothes, Dad wanted to see the new habit. But before I pulled out my first article of clothing, Penny suggested a style show instead.

Taking the newly purchased items into the bedroom, I prepared for the living room style show that would soon go public. My veil and habit had been my comfort shield for the past four years. I had been dressed in the postulant's garb, the traditional habit with a white veil followed by a black veil, and the modified habit. I had not only donned the habit, but the demeanor and molding of each.

"What would the next change of habit to the street clothes of the working class bring to my life?" I wondered.

Removing the short black veil and tossing it on the bed, I shook my head from side to side enjoying the freedom of movement. I remembered getting the veil as a sign of consecration and humility, covering up my hair deemed "women's crowning glory." No more hiding my face and hair. I wondered about the vanity Mother Monica had accused me of.

I unsnapped the white banana-looking collar that had replaced the pure white starched wimple. My black blouse and mid-calf skirt, which replaced the old tunic and scapular, added to the "discard" pile on the bed—a pile of black tradition.

Slipping into a new navy blue skirt and pin-stripped blouse, I studied myself in the mirror. Running my fingers through my matted down hair, I fluffed the brown locks framing my face. The laugh lines at the corner of my eyes deepened in a smile. I recognized a face and figure from years past.

"Where has that girl been hiding?" I pondered.

At home with my family, I wore my new clothes with ease. The discarded modified habit sat stowed in my suitcase.

With one of two tasks done on my annual trip home, I looked for the right time for the second task. Since the day my parents dropped me at the novitiate, I hadn't discussed with them my choice to enter the convent. Were they happy that I elected to leave home and serve God? Would they think me a failure if I decided to leave the convent? I needed to know their thoughts; I needed my dad's approval to stay in the convent or to leave.

The opportunity to talk with my parents loomed ripe one evening. Wringing my hands underneath the dining room table, I sat up straight, unsure of how to launch the conversation. "I need to talk to you about my life in the convent," I blurted out, knowing this subject had been taboo between us.

"What is it, Pat? You're happy, aren't you?" Dad sought assurance, but opened the gate for me to spill my guts.

I gritted my teeth calling on every ounce of strength to be honest with him. Since I hadn't been truthful with myself, this would be a challenge. I took a deep breath.

"I'm not sure about my religious vocation. I'm very lonely. I feel alienated from everything that I knew and loved. I just want to know if you and Mom would be disappointed if I ever left the convent?" I stammered, jittering my knee up and down, waiting for the bomb to go off. My future loomed in front of me teetering on Dad's reply.

Silence hung over the table. My dad eyed me, assessing the accuracy of what I had said. My sight darted from Dad to Mom to pick up any hint of their feelings, their poker faces revealing nothing. I clasped my hands together under the table to occupy them. Finally, my dad broke the silence.

"If you stay in the convent, Pat, I would be the proudest father," he said, putting a slow emphasis on each word reinforced by his brown eyes. "But if you left the convent, I would be the happiest father in the world."

Like I'd done with Father Payne's words, I repeated them in my head. Dad would be the proudest, or Dad would be the happiest.

Choking back the tears, I gurgled, "I thought that you would be mad at me because you told me to try college first, and I insisted on doing it my way. I always did opposite of what you said, and it made you angry."

"No, I'm not mad," he explained wiping his eyes with his handkerchief. "Your mother and I just wanted you to be a little more mature than you were for such a big decision. That's all."

My parents had released me. I couldn't make a bad decision, not black nor white, right nor wrong.

Armed with new mental freedom from Father Payne who represented the Hierarchy of the Church and my father's support for whichever decision I made, I returned to the convent for the summer. But something still dogged me. Even with my newfound guiltless freedom of making the right decision, I hesitated. Making any decision still skewered me with fear. I feared to leave the convent because that would disappoint God. I feared that if I left the convent, I wouldn't find happiness outside religious life. Just like the guilt, those fears bogged me down in indecision.

I found riding the nun wave easier. Indecision about leaving made me want to procrastinate until I gained some strength for a decision.

As August drew near with the time to renew my vows, I took the easy route. Rather than forge ahead with a decision that might have consequences I couldn't tolerate, I opted for the familiar. Despite my growing doubts, I renewed my vows of poverty, chastity, and obedience for two more years. I just wasn't ready yet to cast off God's calling. I just couldn't walk away. Besides, I found the Salix house comfortable with only four nuns. Almost like home.

We had the summer to adapt to seeing each other—the Sisters—dressed in the habit of the poor working class. I channeled my energy forward to planning for my classroom the upcoming fall. In spite of the lingering cloud of discontent, I counted the days until I could return to Salix, anxious to see what my second year of teaching would bring.

Secret Four

Don't worry about making a good decision;
instead, make a decision good.

MY REFLECTION

All my life, most decisions had been made for me: what to wear, what school to attend, what kind of career I should pursue, when to eat meat, or what movies to see. Years and years of ingrained expectations of success and pleasing authority framed every decision I made. When Father Payne told me to focus on making a decision good, I felt like the weight of the world had been lifted from my slumping shoulders. I discovered the freedom of not having to make the right decision or make a decision to please others, but rather to make a guilt-free decision. I could make a choice, and my choice wasn't right or wrong.

THE MORAL WE CAN ALL LEARN

Consider whom you are trying to please when making a decision. If you consider others' expectations of you before you make a move, you may be living your life for others rather than living your life for your own happiness. Happiness comes from listening to yourself and making choices that work for you, not others. Don't worry so much about making the correct decision in the eyes of others. Listen to the voice within, and make the decision with the best of intentions. Then, don't look back to second-guess your choice. Reflecting on your decision patterns will give you insight, but "what ifs" throw you back into the guilt mire. Keep moving forward, being strong with your decision, and make that decision work for you.

Chapter 12

Feeling Naked

Once again, I squirmed about my new habit—this time my street clothes—when we drove up to the Salix convent for my second year of teaching. The single-story four-bedroom brick house with a small chapel appeared to have weathered the hot summer Iowa months undisturbed. In contrast, the four of us arrived in our individual clothes of the poor working class, with no veils and the modified habits left behind at the Motherhouse.

When Father Potter arrived at the convent to plan the Sunday Mass, he swept his eyes across us, taking in our new attire. He said nothing, but dropped his vision to the Bible in his hand.

"Sister Mary Patricia, could you please read the first Bible selection at Mass tomorrow?" Father Potter kept his eyes averted as he addressed me. I blushed in response to his discomfort.

I writhed with that same embarrassment while reading my assigned selection the following day at the lectern in front of the entire congregation. Eyes, like razor darts, pierced through me. I felt stripped—stark naked. My vision locked in on the words of the scripture in front of me. My voice rose in pitch while I attempted to slow down the pace to control the racing on the inside. I steadied the runaway oral delivery and stood tall, concentrating on the message. Missing the point of the scripture passage that I read, heads turned in whispers. Their stares reminded me of my first reaction to seeing Sister Christine's red hair when she modeled the modified habit. Following the service, parishioners greeted us as we filed out of the church to head to the auditorium for the routine post-Mass coffee and donut social gathering. They hurried past us, dodging our eye contact as if pastries were on sale. Our change of habit collided with their inflexible parameters of what a nun should look like, their painful silence sidestepping the question of our new dress and what that meant.

"I feel like people are gawking at me," Sister Mary Sylvia whispered.

"They ARE staring at all of us. I feel like I'm in a parade. Can we skip this scene today?" I pleaded, wanting to hide in the safety of the convent.

"No, we just have to give them time, and they will come to understand that we are nuns from the inside out. The habit doesn't make the nun," Sister Mary Sylvia put a hopeful ring in her voice. Since she had been wearing the traditional habit longer than me, I wondered if she believed her own words.

Not only did the parishioners have a difficult time adjusting to our new street clothes, but we did also. Physical cares that we had relinquished years ago, like styling our hair, were now of concern. Mirrors, curlers, and hair spray became part of our daily lives. Even walking in new shoes—sleeker, thinner, more fashion conscious heels—had to be re-learned. A variety of apparel lined our closets instead of a single tunic. We awoke to choices every morning with our attire even matching our activities: Floral dresses, professional suits, walking shorts, and culottes altered based on the occasion.

We unveiled our new casual clothes at the annual altar boy picnic. We prepared the hamburgers and hot dogs, while Father Potter took the boys fishing at the lake. In warm autumn sun, we relished wearing our shorts, tees, and sandals for the first time.

Sister Sylvia, picking up a package from the cooler, took two steps before screaming, "Ouch!" Grabbing her foot, she hopped on one leg. A char of a broken pop bottle glass stuck through the bottom of her new sandal. Blood oozed from her foot.

Shoving my oversized hamburger spatula to my assistant altar boy, I grabbed the nearest towel to staunch the red stream gushing from her foot. My limited experience as a Candy Striper came back to me as I applied pressure on the cut to stop the bleeding.

"I heard the screaming. What happened?" Father Potter came charging to our campsite kitchen with fishing pole in hand. He glared at the red stained towel on Sister Sylvia's foot. My stomach lurched reading the disgust written on his face. But not taking the time for a reprimand, he turned toward the vehicles, muttering, "I have a first aid kit in my car. I'll get it."

As he scurried off for medical supplies, Sister Sylvia looked at me and laughed. "I can read his thoughts," she snickered, pulling the piece of glass out of her new sandal. "He's thinking, 'You are suppose to be here to help and now look at you.'"

Father Potter cleaned and bandaged Sister Sylvia's wound in silence. After he finished wrapping her foot, he stood up, finally lobbing his reprimand at us. "Nuns shouldn't wear sandals," he spat and marched back to the boys, the fish, and the lake.

Time always aids adjustment. Moving our parish toward change and renewal seemed like trudging through a lake of molasses. But over the school year, the parishioners and Father Potter grew accustomed to our change of habit while we acclimatized to wearing them.

At school, I rifled through the packets of work samples piled on my desk in preparation for the upcoming parent conference with Ben Brooks' parents. My stomach churned with thoughts of how disarming Mr. Brooks had been last year. "I sure hope that his wife comes with him this year," I silently prayed feeling my heart rate quicken. Without the habit to hide behind, I felt exposed and vulnerable like prey, a defenseless target for lurking dangers. I set two chairs by my desk expecting both parents.

"Well, hello there. May I come in?" the cheery voice of Mr. Brooks traveled across the classroom as he casually strolled up the aisle between desks. "Wow, look at you," he added in exclamation, taking the chair nearest to mine where I stood. He sat close enough to me that I could feel the cold outside air emanate from his coat.

I blushed, feeling naked without my veil. I scooted my chair back, feeling his body too close. Jade East again filled my nose. I plopped down on my chair before my legs of water collapsed underneath me, my vision focusing on the desk in front of me to escape the magnets in his eyes. Without a veil, using the Custody of the Eyes as a way to hide proved more difficult.

"I like the new look. I mean, I like the change of habit," Mr. Brooks launched his bold words right into what I didn't want to discuss with him.

"Thank you, Mr. Brooks," I bolstered myself to respond. "Your support is like a breath of springtime after this cold winter. We haven't received great reviews for the change of garb," I divulged in spite of myself, my head inching up to meet his gaze. I bit my lower lip for sharing my pent up feelings of frustration with this man. "I shouldn't be sharing my personal problems with you, Mr. Brooks. You are here on a professional call, and I didn't mean to take advantage of your kindness," I unloaded as my face reddened at being too familiar and losing my religious decorum.

Seeing my shame, Mr. Brooks comforted me, "You know, Sister, the people around here don't like change. They like things the way that they are. They're kind of stubborn in their old fashioned ways."

"Thanks, Mr. Brooks. I appreciated your understanding," I whispered.

I picked up the packet of Ben's work but didn't want to talk about the fourth grader. I wanted to talk more about the man, Mr. Brooks. I wanted to know more about him—to know how he became so forward thinking while living amid friends and family stuck in the same old rut.

Not only did I want to know more about Mr. Brooks, but I wanted to talk about me. I longed to ask him what he thought about a young woman living celibate as a nun and what he thought of me. I wondered if he found me attractive. I yearned to engage in a meaningful intimate dialogue. But my religious training won over. I reeled my mind back to educational issues and Ben's work at hand.

After assessing Ben's schoolwork and going over his report card, I concluded the conference by standing up. I wanted Mr. Brooks and his temptation to leave.

"Don't worry your pretty little head over these people here, Sister," He teased as he rose, flashing a big smile. I flushed, but he pressed on. "You keep doing what you're doing, and we'll catch up one day." He gave a farewell wave as he walked out the door. My shoulders sagged. I wanted more—more connection, more laughter, more support, and more male attention.

Once again, Mr. Brooks lingered in my mind. Images of him nagged as my long brown bangs fell into my eyes, and I swept them away. His casual manner, his playful eyes, his broad smile, and his warm understanding heart plagued me with temptation and promises of loving feelings that I had vowed against. I walked down the hall praying for strength and buried my head in my hands in the chapel.

Alone in bed at night, the face of Mr. Brooks invaded my dreams waking me into acute consciousness. Finding no let up from his image in my waking or sleeping dreams, I succumbed, letting the haunting visions of Mr. Brooks loiter in my mind. My body reacted. I wrestled on the bed, turning over on my stomach to seek solace burying my head in the welcoming feather pillow. Rubbing my groin against the hard coils of the mattress, I stimulated my body to a new sensation. Strange tinglings sent me writhing.

Scared, I sat up to stop myself. Although I had not touched myself, I panicked that reveling in the sensation might lead to masturbation—a mortal sin punishable by burning in hell for eternity. "What is happening to me, God?" I prayed for relief, crying myself to sleep.

One of the side benefits of being stationed in Salix had been its proximity to Sioux City, where my Aunt Rene lived, only about ten miles away. Occasionally, I would be allowed to drive the convent car to visit her. In her late seventies, living all alone, Aunt Rene never seemed to age. She could remember any spoken address or phone number, and her youthful spirit attracted many friends, most much younger than herself. I needed her perspective on my life.

"How do you stay so young?" I inquired, desiring her secrets. "You're not like most older people, crotchety and set in their ways."

"I work at it every day, Patty," she confessed the contrary to what I assumed. "I train my brain to remember details. If I find myself being cranky with people, I stop myself. The way you are when you are young will be the way you are when you are older. If you find fault with things and you're unhappy as a young person, you'll remain the same. You don't change."

At fifty years younger, I felt like the old stooge set in my ways. Mustering my strength to be truthful, I launched into the reason for my lunch visit.

"I'm not sure what to do about my vocation. I'm not sure that I believe in it any more. We are teaching that birth control by artificial means is against our faith. But I don't believe that. And besides, I'm so lonely," I spilled my secret longings.

"I want to be faithful and serve God, but I'm not sure that I want to do it as a nun," I admitted, pushing the food around on my plate.

Aunt Rene took a sip of tea before responding. "The church is changing," she began. "In the future, there may not be nuns as we know them today. With the movement the way it is, I would see nuns as holy women serving the church living normal married lives." My eyes widened at her unconventional vision of the future.

"You don't have to be a nun to serve God," she added in a matter of fact tone. "Besides, you are responsible for your own relationship with God, despite what the church teaches. Sometimes the church may even get in the way of your communication with God," she warned.

"I'm just not sure of anything right now," I interjected. Then I locked my eyes on hers. "Would you be disappointed if I left the convent?"

Her gaze did not waver. "I wouldn't be disappointed or surprised if you decided to leave. You have lots to give no matter where you are."

Aunt Rene bolstered my confidence, her words enfolding me. I wondered if just as Father Talbot sealed my fate to enter the convent over a casual conversation at a family meal, that Aunt Rene had unsealed that destiny over a luncheon table. Kissing my cheek so hard I thought her nose would break off, she bade me good-bye. I drove back to the convent, her words echoing in my head.

Over the remaining months of teaching, I reasoned that I could leave the convent and still lead a holy life that would please God. Not as a nun, but still serving the church. I would not disappoint anyone—neither my earthly father nor my heavenly Father. Absorbing the guilt of duty over the years, my sponge had been saturated. Time had come to wring out the culpability and start afresh.

As the school months wound to a close, I formulated a plan to leave the convent during the summer. Returning to the Motherhouse as usual for summer classes, I intended to talk to Mother Imelda informing her of my decision to leave the convent. I planned to explain my strong desire to serve God and the Church outside the convent. In the spirit of Church renewal, she would understand my desire to help people as lay person and dispense me early from my temporary vows set to expire next summer.

My heart seemed lighter since I made the decision to leave the convent. All I needed to do now, according to Father Payne's advice, was to make the decision good.

Mother Imelda's tall frame, stretching to almost six feet, rose as I entered her office. Her sharp angular face turned to greet me, "Come in, Sister. Take this chair." She turned her out her palm, indicating one of the two seats opposite her paper-strewn desk.

The Mother Provincial donned a dark brown tailored suit with a simple silver cross hanging from a chain around her neck. Other than the lack of worldly makeup and the religious medal atop her suit jacket, she could pass for a bank executive. I stared at her gray hair previously hidden under the veil of her habit.

"It's nice to have you back from Iowa for the summer," she began, pushing a pile of papers to one side and resting her forearms on the cleared area of her desk. "What can I do for you today?"

The gaiety that filled my heart drained, replaced by a gripping fear of my superior's potential reaction to my news. "Mother, I have been in prayerful thought for a long time about my vocation," I launched into my petition, talking faster than usual. "I'm not happy in religious life like I thought I would be. I kept thinking that somehow circumstances would get better. But they haven't. I would like to be released from my vows and live with my family in California."

She eyed me across the desk. "Have you told you parents of this decision?" the Mother probed, wrinkling her forehead in consternation.

"Not yet, Mother. I didn't know how long the dispensation would require, and I wanted to give my dad the exact date after talking to you," I blathered, wondering why she cared if I'd shared my intentions with my parents.

Mother Imelda sat back in her chair, letting the quiet of the room settle into heavy silence between us. The air felt stifling as I sat on the edge of my seat for her answer. After a bit, her eyes pierced into mine with her decision, "Your vows will be up next summer, Sister, and you may leave then without a dispensation from the Church."

"I've considered that, Mother, but I just don't think I can persevere one more year," I confessed, feeling my stomach sour.

Mother Imelda persisted, throwing her strength against me. "I have already assigned you to teach fourth grade here in Omaha next year, Sister. At Holy Name parish." Her uncompromising eyes drilled a hole into me.

She continued, filling the hole with guilt. "We have a commitment to staff the school with twenty-four nuns. If you leave, we will not be able to honor our word. We need you to make our quota of teachers." She hurled a stern warning of responsibility to the church community.

Mother Imelda played the right card. Where Father Payne had released me to make a decision good, my dad had released me to make him happy, and Aunt Rene had released me to serve God outside the convent, Mother Imelda trumped them all with responsibility. She had already assigned my duty for the year as a fourth grade teacher in Omaha, and I could not defy her.

From years earlier when I wanted to drop out of Sister Mary Cleopha's class, I heard the words of my father echoed through me: "God speaks through his representatives. The priests and nuns have a special calling to act as His ministers. We must obey them as we would obey God Himself."

My heart plummeted to the pit of my stomach. I had taken my vows for two more years, which committed my teaching skills for the duration. While I could live with leaving my vows early, I wanted Mother Imelda's permission to do so as the representative of God. I felt like I was back in high school being told to stay in algebra class. I would just have to postpone my departure from the convent by a year.

My sense of duty always trumped my heart, and I knew myself too well to fight my responsibility. I would be the good nun, subverting my own desires, until all my responsibilities were met.

Stifling back the tears, I agreed to the Mother's request. "I'll teach at Holy Name until June, and then I will leave the Order to join my family in California," I whimpered. Like a broken rag doll, I limped from her office. I would do my duty.

Chapter 13

Doing My Duty Again

The long endless summer days at the convent dragged on until at last I reported to my final teaching assignment to fulfill Mother Imelda's business plan. I could have slipped out the door of the Motherhouse at any time to go home to California, but the thought of not living up to my responsibility for the year shot me full of guilt. Not wanting to disappoint Mother Imelda nor God, I wanted to leave with permission, not skulk out like a thief stealing away in the night. I would be obedient to the end.

Moving into the convent at Holy Name seemed like re-entering the Motherhouse, but in miniature. Holy Name convent housed twenty-four nuns that taught elementary and high school. The large austere dorm-like structure stood in as a polar opposite to the intimate home in Salix. The arrangement suited my mood, desolate and lonely. An impersonal chain of command and division of duties replaced the close-knit family organization of the convent in Salix. The large convent, which housed designated nuns for cooking and other household tasks, had no need of my skills beyond teaching. As I blended into the religious fabric unnoticed, keeping to myself, I carried out my responsibilities like a robot—obedient, but mechanical.

Other than Sister Mary Joan, my high school journalism class teacher, the sisters in this convent seemed more as strangers than family. Like a well-oiled machine, the nun cogs taught at the adjoining school by day, returning to the community by night. Interaction with each other kept to polite minimum. Compared to Salix, the nuns remained aloof from the congregation and shunned intimacy with parishioners. Like a good nun, I put in my teaching days—pushing myself to accomplish the simple everyday tasks educating fourth graders. Armored in obligation, I forged into my assignment and added on instructing high school students in religious studies.

But ordinary activities overwhelmed me. After each day of teaching, I drug myself to my bedroom to nap, too exhausted most days to rouse for evening Mass and dinner. I prayed in my bed for strength to get through each day. If anyone missed my presence, no one voiced a word. I ticked off the months like a convict in a prison waiting for the school year's end and the release from my vows. The prison chains of duty and aiming to please held me to my commitment.

In an odd way, I thought my parents and religious community would be proud of me, honoring the spoken words of my vows. I wanted to leave according to the rules when my vows expired, when I had permission to leave. "You must finish what you begin" rang the Camp Fire Girls' motto from grade school. That lesson learned early on was reinforced throughout my upbringing. Thinking that I might want to become a nurse, I became a Candy Striper one summer in high school, but hated every minute of it. I begged my mother to let me quit, but she refused, reminding me that I must follow through on my commitment. But stumbling through my year at Holy Name, no one at the convent, church, or home seemed to care that I was honoring my obligation. I remained steadfast in my obedience to my vows no matter what the cost to me personally.

Trudging through the falling February snow one day, I arrived back at the convent only to have the door open for me from the inside. Grateful that I didn't have to juggle my books and satchel to fumble with the doorknob, I found myself face to face with Sister Mary Joan and an unfamiliar nun.

"Oh, Sister Mary Patricia, come in, before you are blown off your feet," Sister Mary Joan stuttered pulling the door closed to prevent the wind from howling down the sacred halls. Nodding toward the stranger by her side, Sister Joan sputtered on, "Sister Mary Irene and I are working on tonight's liturgy. We were wondering if you would read the responsorial psalm at Mass this evening?"

At a loss for words, I shifted my books and satchel to the other hand and struggled to remove my gloves from my shivering hands to buy time. "I'm afraid I'm going to miss Mass tonight," I stammered. "These teaching days are draining me. I'm just going to bed." I moved to trundle off toward my room, but turned to toss a bone to Sister Joan. "Maybe tomorrow I'll feel better."

Blowing breath on my frosty red fingers, I hoped they would get the hint that I needed to go to my room to warm up. I lied about feeling better the next day, but I hoped that Sister Joan would let me escape without a full-blown interrogation.

"That's a shame," empathized my former journalism teacher. Then, she probed further. "Will you be coming down for dinner or would you like us to bring you something to eat in your room?"

"There's no need for you to do that," I begged, not wanting my solace interrupted by their over eager charity of meal delivery. "I don't have an appetite anyway. Thanks for your offer." Toting my bundles, I inched toward the staircase taking me to the sanctuary of my bed. I may have been deterred by Mother Imelda's insistence for one more year of service, but I held my ground in this bout.

As I turned to leave, I overheard Sister Mary Joan whisper to the other nun, "I taught Sister Mary Patricia in high school. Back then she demonstrated leadership with energy and enthusiasm. We were thrilled when she decided to enter the convent."

Hearing her words, I froze in my tracks hidden around the corner. Sister Mary Irene's voice floated in response, "I wonder what happened to her? I hope that she's not ill. She does look pale."

Shaking my head, I slogged up the steps to the second floor. I crawled into bed, yearning for numbing sleep to dull my pain.

As the year plodded on, darkness clouded around me. I fought it by sleeping. No one in the convent stepped in to rescue me. No one seemed to notice. I wondered if God even noticed my growing despair. The silence accentuated my loneliness and deepened my depression.

While watching myself wither, I still couldn't bail on my obligation. Like a prison sentence, I had to serve my time. I had to do my duty.

My extracurricular task of working with fifteen high school students from the local secular school proved the only bright spot in my dragging gray days. Our after-school class kept them involved in church activities and me in contact with the real world. As I worked to bring religion into their everyday lives, I discovered how much I looked forward to a happier life outside the confines of the convent.

"What do you think about this photo, Sister Mary Patricia?" quizzed an industrious towheaded young man, shoving the latest issue of Time magazine under my nose for approval. Their assignment had been to find representations of Christ at work in today's world. Looking at the picture accompanying a story covering the Vietnam War, I reflected how perfectly the photo illustrated the lyrics to the song, "He's Not Heavy, He's My Brother."

"I don't know how you found such an ideal image, Sean," I praised him, sensing his pride. Sean's portrait of a soldier carrying his fellow wounded warrior across his shoulders to safety visually struck a chord for that tune and moving lyrics.

Instructing this extracurricular class had fallen to me, the new nun on the block. Most nuns considered it the least desirable chore. The troublesome teenagers didn't want to be in religious class following the regular school day any more than the nun teaching it wanted to be there. But the teens lent an unexpected breath of spring air to the drudge.

Being closer in age to the high school students than most of the other nuns in the convent, I found a youthful tie to the outside world that the sisterhood couldn't provide. Lengthy conversations about their lives—including modern music, stylish fashions, and latest trends—brought some outside-the-convent-walls stimulation to my dulled senses.

"Every time I see you, Sister, you are humming that same song we considered for the project a few weeks ago. The one about the rainy days and Mondays. You must like Karen Carpenter," Sean teased me, rifling through more periodicals for project pictures.

Humming the lyrics to the song served as a lullaby, rocking my fits of loneliness into quietness. But the truth extended beyond rainy days and Mondays. Every day spiraled me further into depression. The song gave me a bit of refuge to combat falling headlong into drowning in the whirlpool.

"I like that song for some reason," I told Sean, knowing full well how close to the truth those lyrics portrayed me. As Karen Carpenter's voice mourned her disheartened mood, she touched a chasm growing deeper by the day in me.

Gray days blurred one after the other with no distinct moments of joy. I plodded through my obligations as a somnambulist, sleepwalking unaware through the darkness of despair. Emotional, physical, and psychological exhaustion battered me for so long that I floated adrift in the foulest storm. I didn't eat. I went through the motions of each day, lacking any compulsion to snap myself from my black mood. Entering the convent as a youthful teen ready to say "yes" to God's invitation to serve Him, I struggled to embrace the strange routines of religious life as happiness bypassed me. I had come to religious life on a quest to find God, but He had been quiet. I had come seeking happiness and found loneliness. I had come pursuing the joy of service and stumbled in sadness.

Even as the blackness deepened, I clung to my obedience. It pulled me out of bed in the morning to go to school and drove me through my days. I would be the good nun, obedient to Mother Imelda and God, fulfilling my duty, until the end.

With the California sunshine on the horizon, I counted my last few days until freedom would spring me to the happiness I had known before the convent. I envisioned walking out the door, jumping on a plane, and returning to my home and the joy of my teen days. I imagined chatting again with girlfriends. I saw myself enfolded in my parent's arms.

Now at age twenty-five, drably dressed with a lifeless plain face, I packed my bags in June. Leaving the convent seemed anticlimactic to the momentous event in my life that it represented. The vows that bound me to God as a Bride of Christ dissolved into the air. No signed document or official notice marked my divorce from the convent. The once sacred union was torn apart.

With no intention of renewing my vows, I finally had permission to leave. After seven years, no good byes, farewells, good wishes, or formal closure shut the door on my life as a nun. I slipped out of the convent unnoticed.

Instead of joy peeling at each step away from my prison, I crawled toward California. My shoulders drooped in failure, my feet dragged in exhaustion.

But I hoped for happiness in the secular world.

Patty Ptak, High School
graduation 1965

Sister Mary Kateri,
Clothing Day 1966

Sister Mary Patricia,
Junior Professed Nun 1967

Sister Mary Patricia,
Modified Habit 1968

Chapter 14

Cycling Through Déjà Vu

After leaving the convent for my family's home in California, I floated suspended between two worlds. I tried to leap across the chasm from the religious world to the secular world by making the easiest change first—altering my clothing. I donned miniskirts and bikinis. I looked the California girl.

Loneliness drove me from the convent to seek connections with friends and family, but my high school friends lived in Nebraska and most had moved on with their lives. While I longed for the easy chumminess we had, reconnecting was impossible. Instead, I hung around my younger sister and her surfer friends playing beach volleyball.

With my family, I tiptoed down hallways feeling like a stranger. My family's house was not my home, and my bedroom seemed foreign, no longer containing any of my records or stuffed animals. Even my high school yearbooks had been tossed out.

Standing at the window one day, I overheard my seven-year-old brother Robbie outside ask my dad, "When's Sister Patty going home?" Robbie only knew me as the nun who came for a week's visit once a year. His childhood logic made sense. But at his words, my loneliness ballooned.

"She can stay as long as she wants," responded my dad.

"Will she stay here forever?" Robbie questioned, seeking understanding.

"Sure, she is part of our family, so she can stay forever. She's your sister, just like Penny, Polly, and Kristin."

"So Sister Patty is my REAL sister?"

"Yes, Sister Patty is your blood relative, just like the rest of us. She just served God as a nun for as long as you've been around."

With new knowledge, Robbie broke into a grin. I breathed easier. Although I stung from knowing that my own brother never knew me as his birth sister but as a visiting nun, Robbie's accepting me as a sibling helped me step back into the family.

Other changes, however, came harder. I entered the seclusion of the convent while my peers embarked on opening up new worlds. I prepared for a life of chastity while they met their future husbands. While they joined college sororities and enjoyed social parties, I lived in a sisterhood with designated hours of sewing for recreation. While my peers made their own decisions about education, friends, careers, and marriage, I handed my free will to my religious superiors, submitting to their choices for my life.

After leaving the convent, simple activities such as finding a place to live away from my parents and landing a job to support myself presented insurmountable obstacles. My seven years as a nun taught me minimal skills to tackle the bare necessities of being on my own. Even though I left the convent and dressed the part of the California girl, I was still a nun on the inside. I had been so accustomed to my religious superiors telling me what to do, where to teach, where to live, and what to wear, that I froze in fear, unable to take a step any direction. My dad even had to help me write a resume and snag my first teaching job at a parish school.

Loneliness propelled me to take steps to fit in to the world of normal. Plus, at twenty-five years old, I felt odd living with family when my peers were married, producing children, and getting on with life. I floundered under the pressure to be like them.

Handsome Mark stepped in to rescue me. I slept with him six months after I left the convent in my fast-tracked attempt to catch up to my peers. Of my three vows as a nun, chastity melted away first because I just wanted to be like other girls—doing what they were doing. I needed to rid myself of my imaginary flashing white neon label that proclaimed "twenty-five-year-old virgin."

But sleeping with Mark troubled me so much that I sought confession with Father Dan. A young open-minded nun—a fellow teacher that I befriended—recommended talking to the Jesuit priest rather than going to traditional confession in a church.

When I located Father Dan's small house on the Catholic college campus, my breathing quickened into panic at the thought of sitting face-to-face, spilling my dark dirty sins out to a stranger. As the door pulled open from the inside, my idea of "priest" swept away the instant I set eyes on my soon-to-be-confessor. His perspiration-drenched shirt, a white towel around his neck, and his flushed overheated face announced that he had just walked off the tennis court. If he hadn't introduced himself on the doorstep, I would have sworn that I had the wrong address.

He led me into his living room and took a chair just opposite me while we chatted. He didn't seem to be in any hurry. Laughing like old friends, we talked about my past life in the convent and my new teaching job.

Then without warning, the Father picked up his long purple stole that had been hidden on the table behind him, kissed it, and placed it around his neck. My heart almost stopped. The religious stole meant the beginning of my confession. Walls seemed to close in on me as I tried to steady my breathing.

"You may start your confession," he said, looking squarely at me. My face flushed. I had never gone to confession in an open room. Confession was supposed to be a private affair between God and me—always spoken to a veiled window as I sat in a dark, small closet. My eyes darted around the room looking for a safe place to stare, and I squirmed while my mind raced to find the right words.

"God, are you there? It's me again, Patty. I need courage," I begged in silence. Then, I began as I had so many times before, "Bless me Father, for I have sinned." I paused for a seeming eternity then blurted out, "I slept with my boyfriend, Mark."

There, I had said it. Now, Father Dan could give me my penance, like saying some "Hail Marys" or "Our Fathers." He would dispense my absolution, and I could escape the confines of this humiliating situation.

"Did you intend to commit a sin against God when you slept with Mark?" Father Dan's question made me jolt.

"I love God, and I love Mark. I didn't want to hurt either of them," I said, trying to look him in the eye without fainting. "Things are moving so fast, Father. Mark is four years older than me and wants sex. He talks about marriage, and it's been such a short time since I've known him. He asked me to marry him, and I told him that I've had purses longer than I had known him. But that hasn't dissuaded him. He keeps after me."

"Are you going to marry Mark?" The Father probed further.

"I probably will marry him. My younger sister, Penny, is already married and has a baby, so I think I'm ready for the next step," I assured him. "I'm three years older and feel a little behind my peers. I'm trying to fit in, feeling the pressure to get married and start a family like everyone else."

The Father returned to his original line of questioning. "Knowing that you love Mark, and intend to marry him, do you think that you committed a sin?"

My mind spun with all the ramifications of his questions. Would he kick me out of the church for this mortal sin? Would he tell me not to see Mark if he led me to a sinful life? I just wanted him to tell me the answer, not ask me questions. "I just don't know, Father," I lamented.

I sat looking at the floor and waiting for my penance. But abruptly the Father removed his stole, set it on the table, and stood up. I dropped my mouth open in surprise.

"We're going over to the university for a while," he announced as he led the way out the front door and over to the college. I wondered if Father Dan was going to plant my sinful butt on the university steps wearing a scarlet letter to warn other students. But instead, we ended up in the religious studies department of the school library.

Father Dan perused the reference books, aisle by aisle, pulling out huge volumes as he went. Choosing several large tomes, he piled the books on the table, saying, "This should keep us busy for a while."

Opening up the first volume, he flipped to a particular section and scanned over the page. "Here, read this," he instructed.

My eyes latched onto the title in dark bold letters. FORNICATION. I placed my hand over the big implicating headline in hopes that other students would not spot damning subject matter.

After I read the page, he inquired, "What do you think? Did you commit a sin?"

"Well, I'm not sure," I equivocated. My words sounded trite after reading the lofty empirical study of fornication.

The afternoon melded into a parade of analyses about fornication. Father Dan shoved a book at me, I read, and we discussed sin and intent. I scoured the works for the meaning, questioned the sin, and plunged into the quagmire of opinions in the religious swamp. Good Catholics that I knew slept with their lovers, but I wondered if they had to wade through this mire. Here I was, free of the convent, but ill-equipped to make everyday decisions, including answering Father Dan's questions.

After a couple of hours, stacks of volumes piled neatly on the library table, a testament to the intensity of our study session. Finally, with my eyes lowered, I uttered, "Father, I don't think I've sinned." I glanced up, bracing myself for his condemnation in typical Catholic judgment. Standing up from his library chair, the Father pushed the stacked volumes aside while pronouncing his final verdict: "Then you don't need absolution from me for a sin that you never committed."

"Really?" I contested in skepticism, raising my eyebrows.

"You've just read what the scholars wrote on the subject. You didn't have the intention of turning from God or hurting anyone."

My shoulders relaxed. In the midst of my new chaotic world, Father Dan had shown how to apply the heart and spirit of the rules—a far cry from the Chapter of Faults and the letter of the law of the convent. The weighty burden of Catholic burn-forever-in-hell sin and guilt began to lift.

I married Mark fourteen months after leaving the convent. Dad walked me down the aisle although he had advised me not to marry Mark.

"Why don't you wait? You need more time to figure out what you want to do," Dad begged me over and over, hinting at my apparent immaturity. Dad had used the same reasoning when he didn't want me to enter the convent. But with Dad's admonition hanging like a black cloud in my mind and a nagging in my stomach that I ignored, I walked down the aisle.

To all appearances, I was adjusting in the perfect marriage. But so often practice does not make perfect; sometimes repeated behaviors become habits instead. While I practiced humility in the convent, I failed to develop self-confidence. While I practiced obedience, I lost decision-making skills. I walked out of the religious convent and right into the convent of an unequally yoked marriage.

Much like I had done with Mother Monica and Mother Imelda, I handed over the reins of my life to Mark. I slipped into his life with little disruption. His life became my life. Since I had no real friends of my own, only acquaintances at the school where I taught, his friends became my adopted friends by marriage. His apartment became my home. I cheered for his college football team feeling no allegiance of my own. I took up water skiing because that was Mark's sport of choice.

I hopped from my father's house, to my heavenly father's house, and then to Mark's house. My dad used to thunder, "When you're under my roof, you'll abide by my rules." That philosophy applied to the convent and Mark's house as well.

Like my father and my superiors in convent, Mark took care of me. Just like in the convent, I didn't have my own money, a checkbook, or a credit card. My paycheck from teaching went by direct deposit into Mark's account, so I never even knew how much I got paid. When I needed money, I asked Mark for it.

"Hon, I need some money for Mom's birthday present," I told him.

"How much do you need?" he responded, reaching for his checkbook.

"I'm not sure. Probably not more than fifty dollars." I didn't really know how much I needed until I went shopping to pick out a present.

"Give me a specific amount," he pushed, bossing me like our money was his private stash.

"I worked for that money, too, you know," I mentally sparred with him, but kept quiet. I felt like a child awaiting my allowance from my parents. My vow of poverty slid right into my marriage, just in a different form. I'd traded financial dependency on my father and the convent for dependency on Mark.

Despite our Catholic wedding, Mark's idea of practicing our Catholic faith differed from mine, especially with attendance at Sunday Mass. He practiced his religion as a holiday Catholic going to church only on Christmas and Easter.

"Why don't you come to Mass with me this morning? I hate going by myself," I begged, pulling on my nylons while Mark rolled over in bed.

"Then don't go," Mark lobbed back.

"You should go. You are Catholic, and we are supposed to go to Mass every Sunday. It's a commandment. Keep holy the Lord's Day," I spouted back, reminding him of our responsibilities. Inside, I felt like he let me down in our commitment of a Catholic marriage.

"I don't need to attend weekly Mass, but if you need to go, then you'll have to go by yourself," Mark finalized the debate by rolling back over in bed. Instead of attending church with my husband, I sat in a pew by myself next to handholding couples and families blessed with darling children. Every Sunday, familiar waves of isolation flung me back to my chapel stall as a novitiate.

Instead of poverty, chastity, obedience, I had promised now through my marriage vows to love, honor, and obey. Obedience. The same theme wove through both sets of vows to God and to Mark. "It's my way or the highway," Mark was fond of saying. My response was to please. I felt like a chameleon assuming another's skin.

Flickers of déjà vu began to surface. The video of my life ran on replay, merging together obedience to my father, the priests whose words shaped my path into the convent, Mother Monica, Mother Imelda, and now Mark. None had given me freedom.

Rather than drown in my unhappiness, I grabbed for a lifeline with children. With my sisters having no trouble with conceiving their two and three kids, I expected to have an immediate family. But Mark and I had no such luck. We resorted to several fruitless years of fertility tests, drugs, and invitro. We finally pursued adoption. In the past, I had been so angry with the Catholic Church for ruling out the use of the birth control pill, but now I found myself of the other side, wanting girls to have babies for couples like us who relied on adoption as the only way to have a family.

"Is this a strange twist of fate or is God punishing me for not staying in the convent?" I mused, searching for a reasonable answer. My stomach knotted thinking that God would be out to get me because I displeased Him.

Despite my unhappiness, I plastered a smile on my face. I'd already failed in my marriage to God in the convent; I couldn't face a second failure in my earthly marriage. Besides, I was supposed to be happy knowing full well Catholics don't divorce.

Chapter 15

Facing D-Day

One day at my manicurist's salon, I pulled out vacation photos from our recent trip to Mexico. While waiting for the fuchsia polish to dry, Billie flipped through them.

"Did Mark go?" Billie asked.

"Of course, he went with me," I shot back with a guffaw.

"Oh. Well, he's not in any of these pictures, so I just wondered where he was."

I glanced at the photos in Billie's hands. Mark had opted to sit in the room watching television, while I made new friends around the pool.

"Did you have a good time?" Billie pushed on.

"Absolutely. We had a great time."

"But did you have a good time with Mark?"

I didn't answer. I couldn't answer. I didn't want to answer. But deep inside, I knew that I had a good time in spite of Mark and not because of Mark.

The tiny seedling of unhappiness, once acknowledged, grew like a weed taking over the entire garden of my life. Everywhere I turned, consuming sadness sprouted. I wondered what I ever saw in Mark, the "good catch."

Working up my courage to confront Mark one Sunday afternoon, I cheeped out in a timid voice, "Mark, I think we need to go to counseling."

"What's the matter? Aren't you happy?" Looking startled, he lowered the newspaper he'd been reading.

"I'm not sure what's wrong, but I need to talk to someone," I confided, hoping that he would be supportive and accompany me as I worked through my emotions.

"Well, I'm happy. But if you have a problem, then find a counselor and go yourself," he brushed off my faint-hearted call for help and returned to his newspaper.

Mark lay snoring in bed that night unaware of my unhappiness. I sat wide-awake performing math calculations, trying to assess when he might die and how old I would be.

"What are you thinking!" I berated myself for such dark thoughts.

"I only wondered if I would have any years without him to be happy," I shocked myself at how deep my unhappiness had grown to the extent of counting the years of happiness after Mark's demise. I really didn't want Mark to die, but I couldn't see any other way out of my unhappiness.

Most people who are unhappy in marriage go through a divorce, rather than await death as a solution. But divorce was out of the question. No one in my family had ever been divorced. I didn't even know anyone who had been through a divorce. Divorce was against the Catholic Church. The vows I took when I married Mark were not the temporary vows that I had walked away from in the convent. I pronounced love until the end, "'til death do us part." So I continued to play the good wife.

Just like I did in the convent, I tried to tough out the marriage, thinking that my feelings would improve. But finally, I succumbed to what I had been avoiding. Mark didn't have a problem; I did.

Even with this major acknowledgement, knowing I needed to get out of my marriage, I drifted along with Mark for another two years, trying to work up courage to stand up for myself. The deep-seeded pangs of guilt once again grabbed hold of me. The guilt that kept me pinned to being a good daughter, a good Catholic, and a good nun now coerced me into being a good wife, no matter what I felt.

While I prepared for yet another exit, I displayed the same robot-like dutiful behavior as my last year in the convent. I "walked the walk," but my actions were devoid of heartfelt meaning. I celebrated Mark's birthday, letting it be a reason to continue drifting along in the marriage. I even saved up money to buy Mark a small diamond ring for our twelfth wedding anniversary, filing that expense mentally under "guilt gift."

The weeds of unhappiness grew. Not only did they strangle my spirit, but my physical body reacted as well. The scales plunged in pounds. My physique shrunk to a frail twig. Friends commented on how gaunt and unhealthy I appeared.

"Are you sure you're okay?" they hounded me.

"Yes, I'm just fine," I lied.

My physical appearance reflected the turmoil hidden within for years, I really wanted to pilot my own life, but instead I kept handing the steering to others. It was time to stand up for myself, time to refuse to float on the waves of others' agendas. I needed to grab onto my own oars to do what made me happy. Despite what the Catholic Church taught about divorce, I had to get out of my marriage. I'd deal with the church and my guilt later.

Thirteen years after leaving the convent to find happiness in the secular world, I sat waif-like opposite Mr. Dobbs, a divorce attorney. Years earlier I'd severed the bonds of marriage to the church, and now I was planning to sever the bonds of my earthly marriage.

Standing up from his leather swiveling desk chair, Mr. Dobbs came around the desk to escort me to his office door, bringing the business of my divorce to a close. "Do you have any questions?" he asked, as I stood up.

"Well, how long is this divorce going to take?"

"The papers will be drawn up today and served to Mark tomorrow. Then, it should take six months from the day we officially received signed documents."

"Oh no. You can't serve the papers tomorrow," I protested, my expression sinking into horror. I grabbed my chair to steady myself.

"Why not?" Mr. Dobbs cocked his head to one side.

"Because I haven't told Mark yet!" I gasped for air.

Mr. Dobbs crumpled back to sitting behind his desk again. I fell back into my seat.

"You haven't told Mark yet," Mr. Dobbs repeated slowly to let the full implication of my words take hold. "Why not? When were you planning on letting him know that you are divorcing him?" He looked quite bamboozled.

"Well," I stammered, "Mark and I have planned a two-week boating trip to Catalina." Resorting to the Custody of the Eyes, I pled my case. "Mark has been looking forward to the trip for a long time. I'd like to wait until afterwards to tell him about all this."

"Let me get this straight," Mr. Dobbs squared off at me, boring his eyes into mine. "You, who have just signed divorce papers, are looking forward to getting on a small boat and spending two weeks in close quarters with a man that you no longer love and no longer want to live with?"

His rhetorical expression unhinged my threadbare nerves, but I pressed on with my excuse. "Yes, it would just be too difficult to call this trip off." I figured that I had been living in a sham of a marriage for so long that two more weeks wouldn't really matter.

Throwing his hands in the air, Mr. Dobbs leaned back in his chair. "Take your money back and go to see a psychiatrist. You need a shrink, not me."

I sat there in silence, taking in his reprimand, feeling my lunch churning within me. I needed the divorce. Summoning courage, I spat the words out so quickly that I couldn't hesitate with more procrastination: "I know what I want. I do want a divorce. I have put it off long enough. You can serve the papers tomorrow. I'll tell Mark tomorrow morning."

"There is never a good time for a divorce, if that's what you are waiting for," Mr. Dobbs mollified me.

I practiced dropping the divorce bomb by blindsiding my parents that afternoon with the news that I'd signed the papers. "The last we heard you and Mark were happy and waiting on the adoption list for a baby. And now you say you are getting a divorce?!" my dad had protested. But putting their shock aside, Mom and Dad jumped into planning mode to move me home. They would be waiting for my phone call to be picked up after I told Mark.

The next day, I slumped despondent in my kitchen sipping morning coffee waiting for Mark. The java tasted like acid as my vital organs seemed to twist into a taut ball with that familiar feeling from my convent days. I sat at my kitchen counter, but felt like curling up in the fetal position under the bed covers to hide.

"Where are you, God? I really need you now," I prayed.

My task was to pack the ice chests and coolers for our two-week Catalina boating vacation, but instead, I struggled to garner strength to drop the divorce bomb. I had to tell Mark before he saw the papers.

I dove through memories to pluck up the courage to stand my ground. I thought of Mother Monica who sent me to bed rather than let me leave the convent. I thought of Mother Imelda talking me into staying another year in the convent after I had asked to go. I had to find strength to please myself this time rather than someone else.

"In just a few minutes, this whole thing will be over, and Mark will be on his way to work," I bolstered my resolve. I mulled over the two ways he could take the news: as the understanding man that I married or as the controlling, obstinate pig-head that he could sometimes be. I half hoped that Mark would respond as the latter, making me mad enough to stand tough on my shaking ground.

"Oh, good. You already have your coffee," Mark entered the kitchen dressed in his suit ready for work. "Don't forget to pick up extra batteries for the flashlights," he noted, pointing to several yellow legal pads listing supplies for the Catalina boat trip.

I nodded in silent agreement, knowing I had no intention of going on the trip. Regret shot through me at letting Mark down about Catalina, but I had made up my mind. I'd signed the divorce papers, which he would receive today.

Gripping my coffee cup for support, I initiated the dreaded conversation. "Mark, I need to talk to you." My timid words squeaked across the kitchen. Fearful of Mark's response, I stared at the cup of java as if to read tea leaves for help.

"And don't forget to find out about the dry ice, too," Mark continued without hearing me.

My blood pressure rose. I prepared to do battle, to be strong in my resolution. I would not be put off as with Mother Monica and Mother Imelda.

"Mark, I really need to talk to you now," I repeated a little louder, infusing my voice with desperation. My tummy suffocated under the pressure of my words.

"I have to get to work, honey. We'll talk tonight, okay?" Mark tried to pacify me, but edged with agitation at my unusual insistence for his immediate attention. With my stomach twisted like a pretzel, I took a deep breath forging into combat.

"I haven't been happy for a long time, and I need to talk to you," I fired back, twanging a familiar strain in our relationship. "It always has to be HIS way on HIS time," I silently shored myself up against him.

"I know, I know, but can't this wait until later? I have to get to work, and you have to go shopping," Mark pleaded, stepping around the ice chest on the floor to make his way out the door.

Feeling the terror of a squelched scream that no one hears in a nightmare, I accepted verbal defeat and closed my eyes, placing my head in my hands. I was going to lose the battle before it had begun. Like being doomed by Mother Imelda to an additional year in the convent, I would be bound to suffer in an unhappy marriage longer than I wanted. Desperate, I needed to make one more stab at conveying my decision to Mark.

Steadying my shaking hands, I steeled my voice, "I won't be here when you come home from work. I'm not going on the trip. I want a divorce." I stared out the window into the distance to avoid seeing his response.

Mark stopped, spinning around to see if he heard me correctly. I buried my head in my hands. "I can't live with you any longer," I blubbered through a sob.

"You can't be serious!" Mark exclaimed. I had hoped that he would react with fighting arrogance that would then reinforce my decision to leave. But to my surprise, he responded as a loving husband who just failed to understand such drastic behavior.

Coming around the table toward me, he lowered himself onto the adjacent stool offering comfort, "I know I can be difficult to live with, sometimes even a bastard. But I love you and will work on myself to change."

"I love you, too, Mark," I admitted through tears, gawking down at my fluffy slippers to avoid any possible capitulation in looking at him. "But I just don't like you." I crunched my lower lip to nip the pain of the brutal honesty. I could have made the same statement thirteen years earlier to Mother Imelda: "I love God, but sometimes I just don't like the convent."

Deferring work, Mark sat with me for three hours while we talked, cried, and sorted through our lives. Mark pled his case while I prayed for strength to continue on my desired path for freedom. When he realized that I wouldn't be dissuaded, he stood to leave looking dejected and broken.

As I listened to the final click of the door closing behind him, my heart severed in two. I collapsed on the counter and sobbed. "Oh, my God, what have I done?" I prayed aloud, shivering from head to foot. I had never been that honest with a person or myself.

I had also never felt so much pain.

Chapter 16

Putting Patty Back Together Again

"I've gone through two divorces—first God, and now Mark," I wise-cracked to Dad as he trimmed his shrubs. After leaving Mark, I took up temporary residence in my parent's guesthouse behind their main home. Living a solitary life for the first time gave me time to reflect, to heal, to start my life over again.

"God was much easier to leave," I chattered from the lounge chair. When I left Mark, the teary scene upset me for weeks, wringing me of emotion and leaving me numb. Just the opposite happened when I walked out of the convent. God was silent, almost understanding. Dad shook his head in amusement, and we both snickered at the absurdity.

The past month had settled into quiet, almost convent quiet. I grieved over my failures: my twelve-year marriage, my seven years as a nun. The two decades seemed wasted.

Sequestered in the guesthouse, I cocooned myself away from the world, similar to when I walked into the convent. But one thing differed: This time I knew I needed to decompress, to untangle the thread that bound my stomach. I had to look within, not outside myself, for happiness.

Sharing my feelings with someone felt good, so I continued rambling to Dad, comparing my marriage to God with my marriage to Mark. "It's ironic how much more difficult it is to leave someone on earth," I quipped, enjoying the laughter.

Putting words to my journey, I recounted all the name changes I had been through: Patty Ptak by birth, Sister Mary Kateri as a novice, Sister Mary Patricia from Vatican II changes, Patty Ptak again after the convent, and Mrs. Kilmer as Mark's wife. Now divorced from Mark, I had come full circle back to my maiden name, Patty Ptak.

I described just how Sister Sylvia's words about being a nun from the inside out rang true. After departing the convent, I donned modern dress, threw chastity out the door, and traded my vow of poverty to a cushy life, but I still clung to the vow of obedience. Despite dressing California-style and having sex with Mark, I still was a nun on the inside, finding difficulty adjusting to the secular world.

"Are those flowers that were delivered for you from Mark?" Dad interrupted.

"Yep, I'm afraid so," I frowned. "He's really trying to convince me to come back to him. He asked if I would see his counselor next week." I hung on Dad's response. He wrinkled his forehead and stopped his trimming.

I rushed to explain. "Mark said that my meeting with his counselor would be just the counselor and me. I agreed to meet since I didn't have to face Mark."

Dad refocused his attention on the bush in front of him. "I think Mark's seeing a professional therapist is a great idea." Then added a lob. "Have you ever thought about getting some help? Someone to talk to might help in getting over this divorce."

I knew he was right. I did need to talk—talk from deep inside me like I'd never spoken to anyone before in my life.

"I think I'll just stay right here in this recliner until you tell me what to do. I'm not good at making decisions," I joked, but meant every word. "You told me not to enter the convent and not to marry Mark. You were right. I'm listening to you from now on."

"We all make mistakes, Pat, but what I don't understand is if you were so miserable in the convent and with Mark, why did you stay so long in both situations?" Dad looked befuddled, but sliced right to the heart of the matter.

I stalled with a deep sigh before answering. "Even though you warned against marrying Mark and even though I had reservations myself, I think I stayed with Mark because I thought I could make it work if I gave in and tried to make him happy. Hoping that he'd change, I stuck around." Shifting in my chair, I felt that knotting stomach that had become so commonplace for me. Dad just listened.

"I tried to be a good Catholic wife. I just kept so busy with work and friends that I never stopped to think about my own happiness. What could I do about it anyway? Divorce was out of the question with the Catholic Church. And besides, I didn't want to disappoint you," I whimpered, feeling a rush of tears on their way. "You were the one who told me not to marry, and then I screwed up once again letting you down with a failed marriage and divorce." I fought to hold back the onslaught of a deluge, blotting the beach towel at my watery eyes and drippy nose.

"All I tried to do my whole life was to please you and make you proud of me, and all I did was let you down." The flood of tears unleashed. I shook from the admission.

Reaching for his handkerchief, Dad dabbed at the tears welling in his own eyes. Then he looked at me, his soft words wafting around me like the reassurance of a loved one's favorite perfume, "You know I am so proud of you, and you know that I love you."

Silence wrapped around us for a moment. We absorbed the intensity of the bottled up emotions spilling forth after so many years. "But what about the convent? Why did you stay seven years? I thought you said that if you didn't like religious life that you would leave and go to college," Dad dug into old scarred wounds.

"When you and the family moved, my world came apart," I sputtered. "I couldn't imagine staying in Omaha when you had moved. I told Mother Monica that I wanted to leave religious life and join you in California. She thought I was overreacting to your departure. She told me that I was tired and sent me to bed."

"She sent you to bed?" Dad interrupted, flaring with anger.

"But it just wasn't your moving that made me want to leave. I didn't want to live that life…so desolate and lonely. I was unhappy from the very beginning." Even amid the weeping, I felt relief. This was the first time that Dad and I had spoken about convent life, the first time I verbalized Mother Monica's betrayal to anyone.

"Why didn't you tell me all this was going on?" Dad mellowed his tone since I shook with emotion. To control his fury, he folded his handkerchief and stowed it again in his pocket.

"I tried writing to you telling you how unhappy I had been, but Mother Monica made me rewrite the letters," I blubbered, feeling the resentment building up anew after all these years. "She said that you wouldn't like to hear about my homesickness. Besides that, we were told to never to talk, discuss, or write about anything that went on in the convent." I grimaced, laying Mother Monica's rigid rules in the air between us.

"She made you rewrite your letters?" Dad said aghast.

"Do you know how many letters home I had to remake into happier occasions? Almost every one had to be edited and re-written to pass inspection," my words bristled in the air.

Dad thrust his jaw forward as his ire rose. "Last I knew this was a free country," he harped.

"Not in the convent, it isn't!" I shouted, struggling to gain some control of the ragged edges of my emotions.

Dad looked me over as if to assess that I wouldn't break into tiny shards damned by my own words, and then tempered his own anger. "So, if you were so unhappy, why didn't you take the money I sent you and leave?"

Flabbergasted, I gaped at him. "What money?"

His mouth matched mine for a few seconds. Then, his face grew rigid and red. "For the first couple of years, I always enclosed a check for you in case you might need something for an emergency, like wanting a plane ticket home," his voice and blood pressure rose in unison. He paced the yard, putting the puzzle pieces together after all these years. "You never got the money," Dad bellowed. "What happened to all that money?"

He stared at me, and I made a feeble attempt to explain the novitiate protocol. "Living the vow of poverty meant that we didn't have money of our own since our worldly needs were provided for," I struggled for air, smothered by the convent twenty years later. "I never found a check. Every letter that I received had been slit open and reviewed. Mother

Monica never even mentioned you sending any money." But my words turned to mush as their meaning struck home.

I broke into sobs—heaving wet, uncontrollable, wracking sobs that spewed like a burst water main on the street. For seven years in the convent, I thought my Dad had ignored my call for his help. But all the time, he had been there for me. The miscommunication created by Mother Monica's controlled manipulation had driven a wedge between us, and I had let it continue over two decades.

Dad held me in his arms as we both cried for the loss of those years with my family. My pain was unbearable. The convent severed me from my family, and my lack of courage let its tentacles stretch across two decades. But with Dad's arms around me, they finally released.

While my parents and I regained a relationship, I had plenty more work to do to stand on my own two feet. I had to start with my divorce. Other than the attorney, I'd never talked about the divorce with anyone outside my family and now I had to face Mark's counselor.

"Why did I ever agree to this meeting? What will I say?" I badgered myself. Weak-kneed, I waited for the elevator to open at the floor for Mark's psychologist.

In Dr. Bennett's office, her warm smiling eyes met with my fear. Her tall slender stature adorned with a dark navy suit emitted the trust of a professional. My tense shoulders relaxed as we sat like two women about to have a personal chat rather than the intense grilling I feared.

"Well, I've heard all about you from Mark. It's nice to get to meet you. I can appreciate all the hardships you two have gone though," she started, folding her hands on the neat desk. My defenses dropped down a notch, but still on guard to avoid letting this trained psychologist talk me into getting back together with Mark.

"I know how Mark is handling this, but how are you doing?" Dr. Bennett surprised me by asking.

"Oh, I'm just fine," I chirped, tucking a stray lock of hair behind my ear. Her raised eyebrows hinted that my answer didn't pass her judgment, so I rushed to continue. "I'm living at my parents' guesthouse, missing my old routines, my groups of friends, my own home. But I was the one who left Mark, so I guess I asked for it," I added, revealing more information than intended.

"Can I ask you a question?" Dr. Bennett pried, softening her voice. "Here it comes," the warning alarm blared in my head.

"Do you have any intention of getting back together with Mark?" she cut right to the heart. "Mark is on the edge, so if you don't have any desire to go back to your marriage, please let him know your true feelings. Mark is living with hope that you will come back to him."

Her words, "Mark on the edge," brought the horrible scene at the house last week into sharp focus. I had gone over to pick up some belongings while he was at work, but found our beautiful home in shambles. Unkempt clutter, dirty dishes, half-empty booze bottles, and prescription drug containers littered the counters. Someone else—not Mark, the anal neatnick—seemed to live there. The disarray shouted his anger despite how congenial he'd been on the phone. He sent me bouquets of flowers trying to win me back, while his wrath exploded on the house. My guilt soared.

"I'm afraid that Mark could be suicidal," Dr. Bennett cut off my memory with chilled words. She did not mask her worry. "Do Mark and yourself a favor. Let him know exactly what you intend to do. Don't hold any false hopes out there for him."

"Suicide??!" Blindsided, my heart pounded near out of control. Being the guilt sponge that I was, the thought of causing someone to take his own life was almost too much. My posture slumped along with my head, the weight of Mark's suicidal depression on my shoulders.

Time hung, neither moving forward nor backward in the lingering silence. I could go back to making Mark happy, or I could continue to make my decision good.

"No, I have no intention of getting back together with Mark," I trembled, my eyes tearing up with the words. I searched for Kleenex in my purse to counter them.

"Thanks for being so honest," Dr. Bennett consoled me. "Knowing your intent will help Mark move on."

"I don't know if I can tell him again," I eked out, confiding the fear knotting my stomach. "I barely managed to get it out the first time. I just can't face him again."

"I'll talk to Mark this afternoon," Dr. Bennett offered. But then she added, "And you can tell him your decision on the phone tonight." I shivered at the thought, but knew she was right. I had to sever the hope to which Mark still clung. No matter how difficult. Knowing that Dr. Bennett would help Mark allowed me to let go of blame for his future.

With my first encounter with a psychologist behind me, I felt better about meeting my own counselor. I sat on a stiff-backed wooden chair in Dr. Chapin's office, my leg bouncing as I awaited my first appointment. The shabby office with peeling paint and cheap furniture announced that poor educational insurance plans like mine paid for my counselor, while Mark's doctor received substantial private payments. My payment plan covered twelve visits; I assumed I'd be cured soon.

"Good morning, Patty," Dr. Chapin smiled, extending her hand in welcome. I took my seat as she sat behind her desk, her cheater glasses resting on her nose as she reviewed my paperwork. "I see here that you recently went through a divorce."

"Yes, I did," I confirmed, folding my hands in my lap to hide the shaking.

Putting the papers off to one side of her desk, she looked straight at me and asked, "Well, tell me, how do you feel about the whole divorce?" Crossing my legs to keep my jittery foot from bouncing, I whispered in a little voice, "I'm not sure what I feel."

"Are you sad?"

"I guess so." I squirmed in my seat.

"Are you angry?"

"I'm not sure," I equivocated, choking back a little tickle in my throat. I tried to sit stoic, appearing emotionless, hiding behind the mask of a happy face. I could sense Dr. Chapin's impatience at my reluctance.

"I'm just not sure I feel anything," I blurted out to fill the silent void.

Dr. Chapin wound up our session by scribbling notes on her prescription pad. Her prescription entailed joining a weekly group session. I left the office feeling like I had just flunked the therapy because I couldn't tell her how I felt. I didn't want to discuss my feelings. I just wanted her to tell me what to do.

Despite my failure with Dr. Chapin, I promised to give the group session a try. Walking in the group therapy meeting, I found one empty folding steel chair in the circle. The other eight women, already seated, greeted me with smiles.

As my eyes circled their faces, I wondered what glued this group together. The ages ranged from late teens to late sixties. They donned scrappy blue jeans to designer dresses. Some laughed, some wore red-rimmed eyes from tears. "How do I fit into this group," I wondered.

The facilitator introduced me, handing me a copy of a small paperback book. She explained the format for the group—reading and discussing a chapter a week.

I glanced at the book's title. *Women Who Love Too Much*. I scrunched my face at the contradictory title. "How can you love too much? Isn't that what we are suppose to do?" I asked. My question met with nodding heads and smiles of understanding.

"You'll see when we get going. Tonight, just sit and listen. Next week will be your turn," the leader suggested. I relaxed back in my seat knowing I could grasp the expectations by paying attention to the others.

For the next hour, each woman shared some detail of her tragic story. The stories ran the gamut of physical and emotional abuse, unruly children, and alcoholic spouses. I wanted to laugh at the behaviors of these women handling these manic circumstances. Over and over again, the women let loved ones walk all over them, determining their lives. The thread that wove these women together spun from spinelessness. They chose to take on abuse or pray against all odds for something to change. I wanted to scream at their weak, silly, inane behavior, but instead just sat listening with politeness.

"These women are nuts," I thought. "I can't possibly have anything in common with these kooks." I shifted in my chair, resolute that this two-hour session would be the last of my time with these women. But in the end, as always, I couldn't walk away.

The next week as I practiced my story, the same similar pitiful theme resounded. My music waltzed with the same melody as theirs. As an outsider, I found their actions pathetic. But when I put myself in their shoes, I would have made the same choices.

Over the weeks to come, we read chapters of the book together and shared gruesome tales of our emotional reactions to the forces in our lives. Hearing my own voice unfold my story, I caught the familiar refrain that ran as a reprise between all of our stories. Themes of approval, obedience, fear, and guilt. That first day, when I walked into that room judging those wackos, little did I realize that I was one of them.

Week after week, listening, sharing, and reflecting, I sought assistance from the women. Soon, I graduated from the group to a personal counselor. Referrals led me to a doctor who met weekly with me to adjust to life after divorce, to life in general.

At first, I squirmed sharing my private emotions with a man. Birth sisters, convent nuns, and fellow women teachers had surrounded me. I felt uncomfortable talking about my piddly woman's feelings to a man. I feared that my feelings might be cast off as overreactions or PMS, but he took a different tact.

"Patty, there are certain developmental stages that we all go through. Physically we learn to crawl, then walk, and then talk. Emotionally, we also all go through phases to adulthood: first childhood, puberty, teenage years, and young adulthood," Dr. Watkins shared psychology 101. I sat folded in a comfy suede chair studying him and scrunching my forehead to make the connections between developmental stages and my divorce.

"With your upbringing in a strict Catholic home and your formative years in the convent, you missed some important steps in the maturation process," he tied his observation to my life. "While most kids your age were getting laid in college, you were feeling guilty about what you did in high school," he lobbed the first in a long litany at me.

I stared at him, wondering how he could nail my history so fast. Inside, I began to connect the logic, "Yes, yes, I was!"

"While most kids were experimenting with making their own decisions, you were dutifully following the rules," he added.

"Yes, yes," I screamed even louder inside.

"While your peers were rebelling against their parents and bureaucratic authority, you joined the biggest institution in the world," he threw his home run.

"Yes," every fiber of my being chimed in applause.

As he listed reasons for my developmental stagnation, I breathed easier. I hadn't been a complete failure. I just had a few developmental steps to take before I could run.

"Mental health, sometimes like physical health, can be more difficult when going through a stage if it is put off or delayed," Dr. Watkins added, using tonsillitis, measles, and mumps for his examples—childhood diseases that kids breeze through. "Get any one of those sicknesses as an adult, and the pain and symptoms are more intense, more difficult to fight."

For the first time, someone had explained my choices in life without casting guilt or blame. As Dr. Watkins prescribed the plan of action, which he likened to climbing a rope, I felt my emotions step up to fold my hand around the cord. Guilt be damned for bailing out of the convent and my marriage, I prepared to climb to mental health with his help. I primed myself for experiencing those steps I missed growing up.

Secret Five

"Good judgment comes from experience.
Experience comes from bad judgment."
—Chinese Fortune Cookie

MY REFLECTION

After my divorce, moving back home gave me the opportunity to reflect on my two failures—leaving the convent and ending a marriage in divorce. I finally gained the experience from two decades of bad judgment. But I looked at my bad judgment as failures rather than opportunities. Guilt made me afraid to admit a mistake. Mistakes were sins to be confessed and my fault. I needed to shift my paradigm to see mistakes as opportunities for growth.

THE MORAL WE CAN ALL LEARN

We all encounter challenges and make mistakes, and we all can learn from them. The key is to alter how we look at bad judgment. Shift your view to see failure as a mere setback with an opportunity for growth. Instead of wallowing in guilt over a bad decision, redirect your vision and relish the mishap as a learning experience, an opportunity. Staying with the status quo, on the same road with the same thinking maps, will satisfy guilt, but cause an accident with your own happiness. Throw out the old map and veer off the road to re-pattern your thinking. Learn from your experience and let that experience lead to wisdom. Sometimes your greatest failure can launch you into your greatest power. Knowing this purposeful wisdom—that life is made up of challenges—helps us live guilt free.

Chapter 17

Climbing the Rope to Mental Health

As the summer unfolded, I found myself stumbling through Dr. Watkins' advice and went out partying with my twenty-one-year-old brother Robbie and his college friends. A few pitchers of beer and several kamikazes later, and I was in no shape to be the designated driver for the boys as my mother had requested.

Robbie drove us home, dropping off his pals, while I slouched in the back of the Jeep. The towering eucalyptus trees outside my car window danced while my eyes blurred. My world spun.

When we arrived home, Robbie unlocked the door to lead the way inside. I followed, trying to tiptoe. When my heel caught on the rise of the doorjamb, Robbie grabbed my arm, and we giggled like schoolgirls.

"Who drove?" Mom caught us. She eyed my drunken state. "I drove, Mom. I'm all right," Robbie reassured her. I shrank, hoping to disappear into the wall before she could reprimand me.

Mom's head turned to me, her grave expression incriminating me with those blaming eyes. "Patty, you were supposed to be the driver. You're the oldest. I put you in charge of those boys," Mom scolded me for shirking my duties as the assigned caretaker.

"Mom, it's okay. We're both fine," Robbie stood facing Mom. "It's not Patty's fault. John kept buying her drinks. She's not used to drinking like that, so she had a little too much." I offered only titters in my defense.

I wove down the hall through the kitchen. But before I'd moved out of earshot, I overhead Dad say to Mom, "Well, I think we're raising two college kids now." I liked the words much better than the "We've lost her" uttered years ago in Disneyland.

My year spent in the guesthouse allowed time to put family back into my life. I bonded with my brother, Robbie, who was a baby when I entered the convent. My sisters visited with husbands, boyfriends, or children, which let me re-forge relationships.

One of my many self-help books said that if God closed a door, He would open a window. As I shut the door to a twelve-year marriage, leaving husband, home, and friends, I opened up the window to building the family relationships severed by the convent.

But at forty years old, I finally felt the urge to move out on my own. Excitement like the anticipation before Christmas grew as I read the classified ads in the newspaper and checked billboards for apartments for rent. But my spirits sank at assessing the dumpy properties that I could afford: small units crammed on top of each other with motorcycles and garbage cans strewn along the sidewalks.

"I can't live like this," I moaned from the back seat of the car while Dad sat silent behind the steering wheel in front of one derelict two-story apartment.

"Well, you should have thought about that before you left Mark," Mom lashed out, her anger speaking from the never-ending chore of child rearing. The words slapped my face as if she had struck me with the back of her hand.

Shifting my stare out the window to avoid the sting of her words, I knotted inside with the pressure of climbing the mental health rope as it tangled. "Take me home. I can't do this," I broke into tears, hoping that Mom was wrong, and I was on the right path.

I stewed for days, replaying Mom's rebuff in my mind. Mom was right in one sense. I didn't have the money I needed to live the way I wanted to live. My meager teaching salary couldn't support my accustomed lifestyle. Teaching had been my whole life, my only profession. Since my pay depended on a salary schedule rather than individual effort, the only way for me to get a raise would be to go into administration. Principal's salaries bumped up substantially from teacher salaries.

Becoming a principal appealed to me. Being a school principal—as challenging as it would be—seemed more of a career than a classroom job. Working with teachers to steer the educational ship of the school enticed my call to duty. I felt like a piece of a puzzle slipped into place as I tried the image of being a school administrator on for size.

The goal of being a principal felt good. Juxtaposed to my previous decisions to enter the convent or marry Mark, the idea was mine. All mine. No priest planted the seed of responsibility only to be nurtured by my desire to please; no handsome bachelor lured me, prodded on by my own desire to fit in. The call to serve as a school principal sprang from me. I launched into taking evening administration classes to get a Master's Degree.

The house-hunting horizon brightened, too. Mom returned from her weekly bridge game with news of an affordable guesthouse about one mile away. The small cottage sat secluded out of sight from the main house. It came with the privacy of a yard, but without my parents a few steps away. With my meager belongings, I moved into the furnished bungalow with the renewed spirit of independence.

Tackling teaching full time coupled with attending Master's classes at night challenged my mind, limiting the time lonely feelings crept in to fester. New friends and new challenges lifted my days, dropping sands of hope into my life's hourglass.

Although I had settled into my own apartment, had a teaching job accompanied by administrative aspirations, and enjoyed my new freedoms, something still felt amiss. From all my therapy sessions, I could now tap into facing my feelings. I felt lonely.

I called my sister Polly for companionship. Hearing the adventures of her three sons always made me smile. After the usual catching up on daily family updates, Polly inquired as to my new digs, "How's the new house?"

"Oh, the guest house is great. It has everything that I could ever want and more. It's so private and quiet," I bubbled, but then confessed what I really felt. "But there is only one thing: I'm not happy here. I can't live alone. I'm used to being around people."

"That's normal. You just have to learn to be your own best friend," Polly, as usual, offered a boost of morale.

"How do I be my own best friend?" I doubted that I could do that. I had always looked to others for entertainment, always going along with the crowd.

"Think of the things you like to do with other people and then just do them by yourself. Be a good friend to yourself," Polly explained, sounding like the older sister rather than seven years younger than me.

Polly spoke sense. But first, I had to discover what I enjoyed doing. I water-skied and raced boats with Mark because of his passions. Not mine. What did I want to do?

After scraping through things to do that pleased me, I planned an evening for myself. I drove to the beach to run at sunset, following the jog that energized me with endorphins with soaking up the beauty of the ocean. I sat on a rock watching the tide ebb while pinks and reds smeared across the sky. The salty smell of seaweed accompanied me on my ride home, where I prepared a warm bubble bath complete with sipping my favorite wine. I supped on my favorite dinner and crawled into the turned down bed. Relaxing my head into the feather pillows, I reveled at the perfect evening. I had pursued my own joy alone and ate a plate full of its pleasure.

Pursuing my own joy broke the bonds of unhappiness that had entrapped me years ago in the convent and dogged me in my marriage to Mark. I found activities I enjoyed—especially being active outdoors— while growing in spirit and self-awareness.

I continued being my own best friend, planning special things to do for myself, but something still nagged at me. "Was it loneliness? Was it sadness?" I berated myself in the total silence in my home.

As I sat alone, in stillness, scattered thoughts randomly passing into consciousness, I became aware of a stirring deep within. But contrary to my past feelings when my gut twisted up, this feeling came with a quieter voice. I'd never been able to heed its utterance, let it surface, or be spoken. This time, I listened to the pent up emotions while quiet and gravity embraced me. The sober fact hit me squarely in the face: I could function alone, but not in this isolation. My private guesthouse had turned from a silent sanctuary into solitary confinement like the convent. Although now on my own, making my own decisions, the all-encompassing silence struck at me like the sharp daggers of disconnectedness that haunted me for seven years in the nunnery.

Being my own best friend and knowing that I felt happiest at the beach, I chose to move near the ocean. I discovered a small one-bedroom living quarters on the top floor of an office building right across the street from the water. Large oversized windows brought the ocean blue right into my home. Laughter filtered up from the beach, and I could watch people enjoying the waves. Bright sunshine lit up the horizon as if I could just reach my hand out the window and feel the warmth. The airiness stood out in the vivid contrast to the dark confines of the convent and the cottage.

As I toasted my new living arrangement, I sang along with the chirping birds and relished the traffic noises that meant people. The rhythmic slaps of the ocean waves rocked me to sleep. Reminding myself of my two climbing goals to health, I reaffirmed my determination to get that administrative job and to buy my own home at the beach.

Neither of those would come from others. I had to make them happen. My happiness was not a gift to be received from others, but a skill to be developed.

Chapter 18

Reaching Beyond the Church

Margarita glasses clinked around the table. The sweet and sour liquid ran down my throat, and my tongue licked the salt from my lips. Eighteen months after I had begun the Master's program in educational administration, I toasted its completion with my study group companions. The six of us dove into studying, writing, and encouraging each other. We spent so much time together that we fought like siblings and vented over drinks together when we could crawl out from under the workload.

"So what's new with that weird boyfriend of yours?" Chuck pried with a snide grin on his face. As the only male in the group, he frequently made my single life fodder for discussion. Chuck did not approve of Tom, the guy I had been dating for the past year. According to Chuck, Tom was not a guy's type guy with his long blond curly hair complemented by a diamond stud in his ear.

Tom and I met by chance in the parking lot of my apartment when he nearly backed into me with his black Ferrari. An engineer transferred from Wyoming to San Diego, he worked in the office space below my apartment. The package of the irreverent bad boy in jeans, golden locks, jewelry, and speedster for a car threw me. Tom was outside the norm of good Catholic men who donned suits, ties, and short haircuts. Our daily acquaintance progressed from grabbing a casual bite for dinner to habitual dating.

"To tell you the truth, Chuck, all is not right in Camelot. You may have been right in your assessment of Tom. Tom's ex-wife of seventeen years left him, and I'm beginning to see why," I laid the truth on the table, wanting a man's opinion of this relationship.

"Now what happened?" Gail chimed in for the latest installment.

"Oh, it's not something new. It's the same old thing: I'm trying to please him, and I'm having second thoughts." I looked up at Chuck waiting for the "I told you so."

When blank stares met me, I continued explaining, "Remember that psychologist I met at the party last week? We were talking about my marriage to Mark and how I had tried so hard to make it work. We started talking about relationships in general, and he said something that I've been stewing over."

"Well, what is it? Give us the secret," Gail goaded me on.

"He said that a relationship should be as easy as breathing—like inhaling and exhaling without thinking about each breath," I passed on the second-hand relationship insight. My stomach gnawed at how strained my relationship with Tom had become. Tom had suggested that we see a counselor to work at our relationship; I wasn't sure I wanted a relationship that required that much work.

"I think that psychologist guy at the party is right. You need to dump Tom, the sooner the better," Chuck's eyes twinkled with victory at last.

"I just don't know what to do," I stammered out my frustration.

"You need a good Jewish mother," Gail instructed, "where you can do no wrong. She will love you unconditionally, and tell you what to do."

"Sounds good to me, but where do I get one?" I pleaded.

In a low whisper, Janeen put down her Mexican stemware and murmured, "I have a psychic that you can call."

"You have what?" I shouted in surprise. I picked up my drink to steady myself. Our close-knit group discussed a wide variety of solutions to issues, but we'd never broached one that intuitive before. I'd heard of people consulting psychics, but believing in them was against the Catholic Church, so I dismissed them as sinful shams.

"I went to this psychic a while back, and she's great. She's also a minister who can help you with any problem. You can asked her questions, and she uses these tarot cards to give you the answers," Janeen exposed herself further.

The six of us stared at Janeen until Chuck broke the silence, "At least it's a shot. Try it. You don't have anything to lose." The rest of the group nodded in agreement.

"If Janeen—a normal person—saw a psychic," I rationalized to myself, "then maybe I should try seeing her, too."

I made my appointment with Minister Edith, Janeen's psychic. But when I pulled up to Minister Edith's apartment, I sat in my car scolding myself. "Whatever are you doing here? This is a total stranger, and seeing a psychic is against your religion."

"You're desperate and need direction," I zapped back at myself. My stomach muscles twisted into braids as I stared in trepidation at the apartment building in front of me. "Where are you God? It's me again. I don't mean to commit a sin," I prayed.

I located the living quarters on the second floor. I prayed again as the door flew opened to reveal an enormous Afro-American woman. She looked like she had been singing gospel music her entire life. Her broad smile stretching from ear to ear melted my tense shoulders that had found their way up to my ear lobes.

"Come in, come in," she greeted me throwing her arms around me in an unrelenting bear hug. "I've been expecting you." She squeezed the fears right out of me.

Minister Edith led me up the steps to a small bedroom that had been converted to her home office. Dim lights and drawn shades maintained serenity, shutting out the harsh glare of outdoor sunlight.

"I am the pastor of the Community Church of Christ," she began, settling her gaze on me. "I also am a spiritual counselor working with the spirit in your behalf. I'll tape today's session and give you a copy, if that's okay with you?"

"Fine with me," I replied, wondering why I would want a tape of the session.

Opening the smaller top drawer, Edith took out her tarot cards clasping them in her black hands. I stared at the deck, never having seen occult cards before, and my breathing quickened.

Edith bowed her head in silence, apparently praying for guidance as I implored help from above. Raising her right hand she made the sign of the cross in the air, calling for a blessing upon on me. Although everything about Edith, her office, and her session evoked peculiarity, when she blessed me and invoked her prayer, I felt comfort.

"Patty, I'm here to help you find your way. Please ask me the questions in your heart, and we will find the answers."

At that moment, my two prepared questions seemed trivial. I bit my lower lip trying to sequester their triteness.

"Don't be afraid. What questions have bothered you?" she persisted. I squirmed in my chair trying to find the courage to share my personal quandaries with a stranger.

"I want to know if I should continue my education pursuing a doctorate and if the man I'm dating now is good for me?" Speaking in a timid voice, I hoped that she wouldn't laugh me out of the room with such insignificant matters.

Edith didn't flinch a muscle. Instead, she dealt the cards face up like playing solitaire. A quick feeling of being duped flashed through me. I wriggled in my seat.

After only seven cards faced up, Edith's jaw dropped open. "Oh, Honey," she began, "your life has been so limiting, and now this." The silent alarm went off in my head, and my innards began twirling.

Edith continued with her interpretation of the cards, her words describing my life in the convent without even knowing one thing about me. Her insights ripped open scars as she drew parallels into the present. She drew a verbal picture of yet another convent-like life in my future.

"With Tom, you would continue down that same prescribed life. He would dominate and rule over you," she warned. "I see your foot bound by an ankle chain like a noose tied to a tree. You would only be allowed to go in that small circle."

She paused, sitting back to stare at me. Unnerved by her words, I crossed and uncrossed my legs.

"I usually do not give out this dire information to my clients," she shared in a hushed voice, "but in this case, I feel you need to know what would be in store for you. You have been trying to leave Tom during four lifetimes. All four attempts have been unsuccessful, but in this lifetime, you will succeed."

"Four lifetimes! What is she talking about?" my Catholic mind challenged. But Edith's emphasis on success in this lifetime brought water to a parched land.

"So I've been trying to leave him before," I mused aloud, recognizing that my feelings of wanting more freedom from Tom echoed through my past. I'd wanted freedom from the confines of the convent, but upon leaving the convent, I'd found myself needing freedom from Mark's constriction, too. My past seemed to read like a history of exits from one self-chosen prison after another.

Edith moved on to my second question laying out the scenario of getting my doctorate. "If you stay with Tom, he will not allow you to pursue your doctorate. Following the eventual breakup in fifteen years, it will be too late for you. You will regret the decision, if you do not move to get your doctorate now."

"How can this woman possibly know what would happen in fifteen years," I challenged her interpretation to myself. But Edith was right. I already knew Tom would be jealous of all the time required over the next few years for classes—not to mention that the program would be full of men! My head spun at what Edith perceived.

"You will leave Tom, but not yet," Edith proclaimed. "You are not strong enough yet, but you will be someday. Don't worry."

"Don't worry?" I yelled inside. We sat in silence for a few minutes absorbing the intensity of the moment. The whirlwind wound down to normal in the quiet dim room.

I collected myself, stood following Edith's lead, and fell into the ample bosomed, open-armed woman who had just taken me into another dimension. She blessed me again, handed me the tape, and reassured me that all would happen in due course of time.

In the car on my way home, relief welled up. Despite the dismal reading of my future, my questions found answers. Relief fed into excitement, and I felt a compulsion to share the experience with someone. I could hardly play the tape for Tom; he'd be so upset had he even known of the conversation, let alone Edith's response. On instinct, I drove to my parents' house.

With Dad out playing golf, I played the tape for my mother, eager to obtain her feedback. Listening with full concentration, she didn't show any sign of emotion as per her usual behavior. Clicking the button ending the hour-long session, I pumped Mom for her response, seeking a rational opinion.

"Patty, you know that seeing a psychic is against our religion. And so is reincarnation. This is a bunch of hooey," she laid out her answer in her clipped German style. My spirits sank, but maybe Mom was right. Maybe going outside the church's beliefs had been a mistake. I could hardly believe Edith's words myself, but I filed them in my heart—hoping that one day, I would be strong enough to leave Tom.

Returning home to the beach, I hid the psychic tape in my bottom drawer under my old workout clothes. I would enroll in the doctorate program and shove Edith's words about Tom out of my mind.

Secret Six

"When the student is ready,
the teacher will appear." —Zen Proverb

MY REFLECTION

This ancient Zen saying plays out in our lives as teachers appear just when we are ready for them. When I visited Minister Edith, I was taken aback by her jovial, muumuu-clad appearance and her tarot cards. Minister Edith was way out of my normal range for receiving religious counsel, although she had the title of authority being a "minister." But I was desperate and had not done too well on my own within my normal religious practices and comfort zones.

THE MORAL WE CAN ALL LEARN

This old Zen teaching is all about the timing of the universe. It's like a dance of growth, moving in syncopating rhythm step-by-step: ready, set, appearance of the teacher. But in order to be ready, one must abandon judgmental preferences and living by guilt. The readiness and openness of the student is paramount; otherwise, the opportunity to learn may be missed. The teacher may not be a traditional conduit of learning, nor even recognized at the time as a true guide. But the timing is still a pivotal moment. Letting your heart be open to all incoming messages, no matter what form they take, will help to propel you to the next steps of your life. Keeping an open mind will allow you to be ready for any teacher to appear.

Chapter 19

Perceiving Perfect

"**M**a'am, we have two boxes without room labels on them, where should we put these cartons?" the husky overweight moving man asked, hoisting the smaller of the two containers on his broad shoulder in my new house. As the Berlin Wall tumbled down in 1989, symbolizing freedom for 3.5 million East Germans, I heralded in my personal independence with new digs—my own home at the beach.

"That one goes in the master bedroom upstairs, and that one stays right here in the office," I directed as I rearranged items on the desk to make space for the last of the school materials. Boxes littered my new home, but those stuffed with binders, notepads, and pens would claim my attention first. Staying up on my doctorate program work allowed no down time; I had deadlines to meet.

After I signed the loan papers, the long-awaited day arrived. Two years of saving money, living some of that time with my parents, allowed me the necessary down payment to purchase my own house, located in a condo project just up the street from my rental apartment. Huge windows and sliding glass doors faced the ocean with the water almost leaping into my living room. The sunshine beaming in from the west reflected my bright mood and boded a promising horizon.

In contrast to the cold impersonal industrial-looking convent, my small beach house nurtured warmth and intimacy. Marrying Mark moved me from the nunnery into his house—furnished, financed, and managed by him. His stark brown utilitarian shutters now gave way to my billowing pink and green ribbon tied back window treatments. At long last, I found home. My home.

"Isn't this just perfect?" I grinned at the man from the moving company as he shoved his clipboard under my nose for my signature.

"Yes, ma'am, it is perfect," the mover agreed in his monotone business voice.

As the phone rang, I located the receiver behind boxes. My sister Polly's high pitched voice shot through the phone from Coeur D'Alene, Idaho, "Hi, Patty, are you all settled in yet?"

"The moving van just left. Once I get my computer up and working, I'll relax." The pressure of a paper due next week bore down on me, and I reached for the keyboard at the bottom of an open box.

"I bet it will feel better to be in your own location and not above the office space where Tom watches your comings and your goings all day," Polly reasoned, expressing her dislike of Tom's possessiveness. Tom had proposed marriage a few months earlier, which I tabled due to doctoral work. We still dated, but with much less fervor and even less frequency. A heavy load of assignments gave me little time to spend with him.

"Yes, I can breathe a little easier now," I reassured her. However, I knew moving away from my apartment above his work meant an increase in phone calls from Tom.

"Patty, I have the perfect man for you," Polly pressed further on her anti-Tom agenda. My ears perked up.

"Well, tell me about him. What's he like?" My misgivings about a future with Tom kept me on the lookout for Mr. Wonderful.

"His name is Joe," Polly began with the facts. He came to Coeur D'Alene to develop a new golf course, the Coloradan had hired Polly's husband as the attorney to help with utility regulations. "He's tall, about 6'4", has distinguished salt-and-pepper hair, is Catholic, likes to ski, and plays golf with us. He is so much fun. You and Joe are made for each other." Polly raved so much that she sold me on our compatibilities as a couple, sight unseen.

"He does sound pretty interesting. Why haven't you told me about him before?"

"There's just one little thing," Polly's voice dropped a decibel. "Joe is married."

"Married?" I screamed into the phone. "That's just not a little thing, Polly. You must be nuts to think that I'm going to get involved with someone like that." The mere thought of having an affair with a married man stiffened my Catholic spine rigid.

"But, Patty, Joe is married to this bitchy lady. He travels all the time just to get away from her. He's only staying with her for her kids. They're not even Joe's kids, and he is the best father to them," Polly defended Joe's character. "He doesn't know that I called you, but I think you should at least meet him."

"No way! I'm not going to meet him. I have my hands full balancing Tom, my teaching, and my thesis," I blasted back.

"Oh, okay. You're probably right anyway," Polly deflated, veering off to a safer subject. "How's the job hunting coming along? Any new interviews?"

"Nothing too favorable," I admitted. The drudge of reading the posted administrative openings and sending out resumes had dragged out longer than I had hoped. "But on the positive side, I did find this one school looking for a vice principal with my qualifications. I'm going to investigate it a little more."

After satisfying Polly's need for an update on my life, I started to clear my desk to begin my paper for my personnel and contract issues class. Sorting through the mail, I caught a return address—The Archdiocese of San Diego. My heart seemed to stop for a second. The envelope held the answer to my marriage annulment petition.

Since the Catholic religion refuses to sanction divorce, those Catholics who go through divorce have four options: live together in sin without being married, remarry outside the Catholic faith, never remarry, or apply for a dispensation to annul the marriage on grounds agreeable to the Catholic Church. When I divorced Mark, I mollified myself by shoving the whole idea of sin and divorce under a mental rug to deal with at a later date. My standing in the Catholic Church remained intact based on the fact that the church did not recognize my divorce, but the state did. Since my confession to Father Daniel and his absolution in the religious studies section of the library, I remembered the lesson of intent. My divorce did not mean that I turned away from God or his church. I continued going to Mass. After all, Mass was habit.

Two years after Mark and I divorced, I heard through the grapevine that he had been dating again. To me, that signified the time to heal my wounds with the Catholic Church. Even though I had no intention of marrying again, I did want to follow the rules, of course. Gathering courage, I asked him if he would fill out the necessary paperwork for an annulment to our marriage. To my surprise, he agreed. After writing out explanations on multiple forms, answering probing personal questions on paper and during interviews, we waited for the Catholic legal department to weigh our case. A year passed. But now, I held a verdict in my hand.

Tearing open the envelope, I raced my eyes down the letter, seeking the verdict from among the legalese, my shaking hands trying to steady the papers. As if stabbed by a double-edged sword, I had been awarded my divorce, but at a cost. The document read: "Annulment granted on the grounds that Patricia did not enter into a legally lawful commitment because of her limited knowledge and freedom."

The annulment granted me freedom to be a Catholic of good standing and even to marry again in the Catholic Church, but all because of my lack of worldliness. What an ironic turn of events: After years in the convent divesting myself of the materialistic world to serve the church and be married to God, the Catholic Church now accused me of being too immature for the sacrament of marriage! The convent thought that I had been mature enough to become a Bride of Christ, but apparently, years later I lacked the maturity to marry Mark.

I stomped around my study, venting aloud. I sparred with the Catholic Church and all its rules with no one but the walls of my new home to absorb my rantings. Ripping open a new box of file folders, I stuffed the annulment letter into a manila organizer, labeling it "Important or Not So Important Papers." I crammed the file in the back of a drawer and gave the drawer a livid kick shut as if to give the Catholic Church a taste of the insult it gave me.

The ringing of the phone cut into my jousting with the church. Picking up the phone, I shook myself to quell my animosity and avoid snarling at the caller.

"Hey, Patty, Bonnie here," she greeted me, as I breathed myself into a calmer state of mind. Bonnie—one of my doctoral program study cohorts—worked for the county education department during the week while we attended classes together on weekends.

"What's up, Bonnie?" I inquired, forcing my voice into casual conversation.

"Remember that job opening for a vice principal in East County you asked me to check on for you?" Bonnie lobbed, refreshing my memory in my administrative search. As a good friend, she had called to report.

"This job is perfect for you. I know the superintendent and principal well. Both are bright dedicated people. You would fit right in. Matter of fact, the superintendent is using the negotiating model of union bargaining that you are writing your dissertation on. He might even give you some ideas," Bonnie rambled on while I tried to concentrate on her words of good news.

"They are having interviews next week, so get that resume out there," Bonnie encouraged. Elation sent me soaring. But a glance at the calendar on my desk made my shoulders drop as I tallied up the planning, research, and paperwork required to apply for the position—all on top of moving in, teaching during the week, and meeting a time-consuming school assignment deadline.

Putting the rest of the unpacking on hold until after my interview the following week, I lived out of boxes. I prepared for the interview by reading the district documents. By the day of the interview, I knew more about the district's programs, goals, and achievements than most parents whose children attended the schools.

During my administrative job hunt, I appeared in front of a few interview panels. They chugged through questions, stress-filled and conversation-tense. I walked out feeling like I wouldn't fit into the school anyway.

But this interview stood different from all the others. It seemed as natural as breathing in and out, without thinking, like how the psychologist described a good marriage. During the free flowing conversation among the superintendent of the district, two other district principals, a school secretary, and parents representing the school board and PTA, and myself, I saw the pieces of the same educational vision fall into place. Bonnie was right. I was perfect for the job. They agreed.

I would serve as the vice principal the first year for the 800-student public elementary school with the understanding that the following year, the school would divide in half. Then, I would be granted the principalship of one of the smaller 400-student schools.

"Perfect!" I smiled to myself.

Having achieved my two goals of owning my own home at the beach and getting an administrative position, at age forty-three I felt like I had climbed to the top of that mental health rope of maturity. Joy at my own achievements spun the images of the convent deep into my memory.

The annulment rationale still grated on me, but I soon settled for what it granted—that with full knowledge and freedom, I could enter into the holy sacrament of matrimony in the Catholic Church. But marriage to Tom was the last thing on my mind.

Chapter 20

Gutting It Out

"**I** have some great news," Polly panted, her giddy gaiety spilling over the phone line from Idaho. "Joe's divorced! Well, isn't that wonderful for you?"

Polly's words registered as I recalled the perfect man she had promoted last year. I launched into a rebuff of her insensitivity. "That's great, Polly, but Tom and I are now planning a wedding. For November. Remember?"

"I know, I know. But you're getting too old to buy green bananas. You need to hurry up and be happy."

"Oh, Polly, it's bad timing on Joe's part. I had years when I was available, and Joe was married. Now he's divorced, and I'm engaged. Joe might be perfect for me, but I just have a difficult time with these lifetime decisions and have to say 'no' to Joe."

My stomach twisted just thinking about a possible confrontation with Tom about any hesitancy over our upcoming marriage. Tom and I had been seeing a counselor together to get our relationship on a more even keel. After three years of dating, he felt ready for marriage. I stalled. I knew my heart didn't feel settled with him, but I attributed my unresolved feelings to being under too much pressure from diving into my first administrative job and trying to complete my doctoral work.

"But Joe is so wonderful. You would just love him," Polly pleaded one last time, knowing that I wouldn't walk away from my commitment to Tom. I needed to appease my discouraged sister, so I shifted the subject to my next visit.

"Tom and I are looking forward to visiting you in Idaho this summer. We'll stay with you for a couple of days and then a few with Mom and Dad. We'll have a great time." My parents now lived a block from Polly, so a visit to Idaho would mean seeing quite a bit of my family—much to my liking, but not to Tom's.

I hung up the phone knowing how disappointed Polly felt. I looked forward to our summer visit, hoping that Polly would grow to love Tom as much as she apparently liked Joe. Coping with my uncertain feelings for Tom made refuting Polly's remarks even more difficult. Her words echoed over and over in my head.

With my year of being an elementary school vice principal almost behind me, I looked forward to visiting my family with Tom. Part of the family time would be spent planning our November wedding, and I hoped Tom and my family would grow fond of each other. Tom had shared a few holidays with my parents, but he didn't relish the same anticipation as me for visiting them. My family also maintained a reserved reluctance about Tom, but they wanted to support my decision to marry him.

The week before we were scheduled to fly to Idaho, Tom made an announcement: "I'm afraid that I can't go with you to see your parents."

"Why not?"

"Right now, I can't afford the time and the money to be away from work," Tom muttered. His eyes traveled around the room looking anywhere but at me. He shifted his weight from one leg to the other.

I could not argue with his reasoning since I had been so engulfed in my job responsibilities, too. But knowing his job pressure didn't ease my disenchantment with him. The trip would have been Tom's time to win over my family. Deep down, my stomach ached knowing that he didn't like my family any more than they liked him.

"You go and have a good time with your family," he said, hinting at his relief.

Alone and feeling let down, I made the trip to Idaho by myself. Days filled with leisure around Lake Coeur D'Alene plucked the stress from my life. Polly, ever on the lookout for diversions, tossed me a pair of golf socks one day.

"Let's go to the golf club this afternoon and play in the little nine hole tournament. Then we can stay for dinner."

"I haven't played golf in years, and you want me to play in a tournament?" I chided her insanity. Her golf group met for a nine holes and dinner every Friday. I should have been thrilled to be included, but my lack of confidence in my skills held me back.

"It's only for fun, and it's all our friends. Most of them you already know." Polly begged, shoving a pair of her golf shoes at me.

When we arrived at the club, I discovered that Polly withheld certain details of the tournament. The event was a couple's tournament, in which each person hits the alternate shot. Perusing the attire of the other players, I glanced down at my own clothing—my denim mini skirt topped with a jeweled T-shirt. At the lake, the combo made me feel like hot stuff, but it seemed a little out of place compared to the other women's matching golf outfits of appropriate length shorts and coordinated colored polo shirts with turned up collars. Embarrassed by my non-golf clothes, I fortified myself with the thought that I didn't know any of them nor needed to impress them with my apparel.

With teams posted on oversized charts, I joined the crowd of the golfers pressing toward the board to locate their start order. My eyes darted across the predetermined teams on the list—Polly and her husband, Mom and Dad. For a minute, I thought my name had been omitted as my eyes flew up and down the columns of bold printed italic names. Then, I found it: "Patty Ptak" paired with "Joe Kogutek."

The name clicked. I panicked, not only because of my poor golf skills, but I was an engaged woman paired with a single man—the same Joe that Polly had wanted me to meet. Part of me wanted to see what Polly saw in Mr. Wonderful while my saner half wanted to run. Now I knew why Polly didn't warn me about the dress code.

My heart raced at the thought of being set up—especially with Joe, who was in the golf business, and no doubt assumed I could play as well as Polly. But I calmed my nerves knowing that if I golfed with him that I could no doubt put an end to Polly's lobbying.

Polly beamed as Joe sauntered up to my awaiting family, clutching his Styrofoam coffee cup, sipping and smiling all the way. My eyes drew up his tall height; he dwarfed Tom by a good six inches. I stood up a little taller to meet his twinkling gaze.

Leaving his tanned face, my eyes traveled down to his broad chest to his thin muscular legs looking very dapper in his impeccable golf attire. He appeared so suave, but I detected a hint of nerves hidden in his polite, affable exterior.

Joe introduced himself. He extended his hand, holding mine in a secure handshake. My breath quickened at being taken in by his commanding demeanor. At first glance, he was the total package that Polly had promised.

"Let me get your bag." Joe lifted the heavy bag of clubs as I watched his graceful movement. Enrapt with his gentility, I climbed into the golf cart, and he drove us to the first tee. All thoughts of Tom—my fiancée—vanished.

During the game, Joe made a point of putting me at ease with his innate golf skills and knowledge. He encouraged my abilities, carried my clubs, and went in search of the drink cart girl to refresh my empty cocktail glass. I laughed when he told me the story of his round of golf earlier that day. Without mercy, my brother-in-law and other buddies teased him about his blind date with a nun. I giggled at his recounting some of the unkind stereotypic nun jokes they lobbed at him. Joe had been a good sport, and my family loved him. I could see why.

Unlike me, Joe had known about our prearranged golf date. Polly, ever the matchmaker, sold him on the idea of meeting me. Thinking that an ex-nun and a non-golfer couldn't be that bad, he agreed to the date. But he never foresaw his teammates during the morning's round of golf disconcerting him so. By the time he finished the morning round, his feet had cooled about the date with an ex-nun. Rounds of rum floats brought him out to face me at that first tee. He shared his uncertainties so casually with me, while letting me know that I didn't come close to one of their jokes.

After our tournament, I sat next to Joe that night at dinner with the other golfers, both family and friends. We bantered, laughed, and blamed Polly for our lousy score.

"See, I told you that you would like Joe," Polly triumphed in the car on the way home, gloating like a proud mother. I had to admit that I did have a great time and did enjoy Joe. But the nagging thought of Tom shot a spike of guilt through me. I dismissed it knowing that Tom had been invited to Idaho, too.

The following day most of the same group rallied their boats on the lake like a flotilla. Being the lone outsiders, Joe and I were thrust together. We talked and swam, enjoying the lake for a day sprinkled with water sports.

Since Joe knew all about my family, having been golfing with them on his many Idaho visits, we chatted like old friends. He shared stories about his marriage and divorce while I talked of the convent, Mark, and Tom. I found myself opening up, revealing detail after detail of my emotional past. I felt like I babbled, but Joe held onto my words no matter how silly they seemed to me.

As the day ended, Joe asked if he could take me to dinner the following evening. Catholic guilt reared up, but I squared off against it. I set aside my uneasiness by assuring myself that it was a harmless meal with a friend, rather than a date. "I had to eat, didn't I?" I rationalized, feeling the tugs in my stomach as I squelched thoughts of Tom.

"Now, you two be good," Polly admonished when Joe came to pick me up for dinner. Overcome with just how handsome Joe seemed, so impeccably dressed, I giggled with shivers. My face flushed catching Joe's admiring gaze as he came into Polly's kitchen to clean his sunglasses. I took a deep breath feeling like a young schoolgirl going on her first date, my tummy doing flip-flops.

When I returned to Polly's house about 2:30 a.m., Polly sat on my bed. Her taut face muscles relaxed at my appearance.

"Where have you been? Are you all right?" she demanded. "Well, how was it? Do you still like Joe?" She pounded question after question until I interrupted her.

"Remember how I told you that he might be Mr. Wonderful?" I lured her in. She sat up bright-eyed waiting to relish in details. "I just have to tell you that Joe is not Mr. Wonderful anymore," I dropped my eyes lowering my voice to a hush. Alarm spread across Polly's face.

"What happened?" Polly slumped down on the bed.

I sat very still looking droopy eyed out the window into the darkness of night. I whispered, "Joe's not Mr. Wonderful." Then when I saw the full effect of my words smother Polly, I threw my arms in the air, exploding, "He's Mr. Perfect!"

Polly jumped up on the bed and started dancing like a youngster. "I told you so, I told you so."

We sat like two college girls on a dorm bed as Polly glued her attention to my words, not missing one detail of the night. I described Joe's kindness to everyone he met, and the staff rapping softly on the door as not to disturb our dancing and our endless conversation. I lingered over his chivalry—opening every door, pulling out my chair, rising whenever I entered our private dining room. I had never felt so accepted. His gentle caring ways and twinkling eyes swept me up in their embrace. By the end of replaying the memorable night, Polly and I lay drained from the sheer emotion.

"He's just like breathing, Polly. Easy, so easy," I mused aloud.

The euphoria dissipated the next morning with the images colliding of two men in my head—Joe and Tom. I was falling in love with Joe, but planned to marry Tom.

But had I learned something from the convent and marriage to Mark. I learned to listen to myself.

Without needing to know Joe's intentions, I knew what I had to do about my future plans to marry to Tom. I had to go with my gut feeling, no matter how much the consequences would hurt. If I didn't, the pain would be worse later.

With trembling fingers, I dialed Tom's number half hoping he would not answer the phone. We had spoken last several days ago, and a lifetime seemed to have passed since then. With each ring of the phone, my knee jittered more while I bit my lower lip.

"God, are you there? I really could use a lot of help with this one." I prayed in silence to find the needed courage, counting the rings until I could hang up.

"Hello," Tom's deep familiar voice finally answered.

"Hi, Tom," I squeaked out, sounding despondent, rather than

elated to talk to my fiancée. My eyes shot to the floor, displaying the old Custody of the Eyes, as I spoke.

"I tried to reach you a couple of times, but you didn't pick up," I blundered around with how to launch into my decision. Trying to sound as normal as possible, I forced my voice into cheeriness, but my heart pounded so loudly that I thought he might be able to hear it thumping through the phone lines.

"I went wind surfing in Cabo for a few days with my buddy, Jake. I figured since you were gone, it would be a good time to get away with him. He has been after me to try the waves in Mexico." Tom sounded somewhat on edge himself, his words revealing more about his choices than he'd intended.

Irritation at his choice to go surfing rather than meet my family helped me gain the upper hand. I took a deep breath and gushed out my message: "Tom, the wedding is off. I can't marry you in November."

"What do you mean? What in the hell is going on up there?" His anger shot up.

I fumbled to explain the whole messy situation as best as I could. "I met this guy, Joe, up here. I don't know if I'll ever see him again after this week, but I enjoy being with him. My gut keeps telling me that if I feel about Joe the way that I do, then I shouldn't be marrying you. I have to start listening to the emotion that keeps talking to me. I haven't been very good at it my whole life, but this time I'm listening to me. I'm so sorry."

The phone went dead in my hand. I sat weeping wondering if following my gut would ever bring happiness.

Secret Seven

Happiness is not a gift,
but a skill.

MY REFLECTION

My life had been a search for God and happiness. I believed that God made me to "know Him, love Him and serve Him and to be happy in this life and in the life to come" (according to the old Baltimore Catechism). I had been looking to my family, God, his church, the convent, Mark, Tom, and others for my happiness. Guilt kept me clutched in the enticing trap of depending on others to make me happy. I saw others' happiness and marveled at their blessed gift, but failed to realize that happiness is a skill to be developed, not a state of mind that is bestowed on one. I thought that if I could follow the rules and keep everyone happy that I would be happy. How misguided I was!

THE MORAL WE CAN ALL LEARN

As humans, we are endowed with the ability to gain the skill of happiness. On the outside, it looks easy. But we often chase happiness down the road of life, always looking to a future time, place, or event. There's no better time to be happy, but now, this moment. To gain the skill of acquiring happiness, learn to live in joy. Begin by looking "within" rather than "without." Then, shun the guilt behaviors that keep you bound from happiness, remembering that happiness is an "inside job," sometimes gained through adversity. Seek out what gives you joy and pursue it. Follow your bliss. Learn what makes you happy—what makes your soul sing. There you will find guilt free happiness. There you will find God. Amen.

Chapter 21

Embracing Happiness

As the flight attendant passed through the aisle to collect the remaining beverage service debris, the plane neared its final approach into Stapleton Airport in Denver. I sat back reminiscing about the last year. When I returned home to San Diego after my whirlwind Idaho visit, meeting Joe and breaking up with Tom, a new sense of self-empowerment energized me. I felt confident in facing my future.

Looking back over the years, I saw that my survival mode urged me through a journey laden with self-discovery and spiritual awareness. Personal growth had been a slow messy road for me—like a street full of land mines with explosive exits. I'd bailed on two marriages, one to God and one to Mark. Shaking my head, I wondered how I'd let others paint my roadmap for me into the convent and marriage. Then, with Tom, I blundered with my own map to another bad exit.

But instead of being steamrollered by the pattern of turmoil in my life, I sat on the plane on my way to meet Joe with a sense of reconciliation with my past. I had settled my past with myself.

After leaving Joe in Idaho, I had no idea if he would ever call. I yearned to spend time with him, but I also felt content enough with myself even if he never contacted me again. I had discovered peacefulness in being by myself. I was going to be okay, no matter what. I had grown a long way from that high school teen always trying to please and to do the right thing.

After leaving Idaho, Joe did call. Joe did call that night. And Joe did call every night after that. Although he lived in Denver and I worked in San Diego, our relationship grew in spite of the miles. On his way overseas for his job, he connected his flights through San Diego, and during long weekend holidays, I flew to Denver. This geographical space, although a hurdle in the relationship, gave me the time to complete my doctorate and develop my skills as an elementary school principal.

Walking into the Denver terminal, I spotted Joe standing in his habitual location far off in the back of the waiting area. He hung in the back so his height wouldn't block someone else's view. My heart raced as I hurried his way, grinning back at his smiling welcome. With his arms wrapped around me, I could almost feel the beating of his heart as he kissed my lips.

We lived like hermits most of the weekends with long walks and extended dinners, only to be distracted with an occasional party meeting a few of Joe's closest friends. The ease of our conversations flowed as between soul mates. I didn't have to stop to explain what I had just said or how I felt. Joe understood. His Catholic upbringing in a severe family with inherent values similar to mine put us on a level playing field. Communication was easy, like breathing. I smiled, remembering the words of the psychologist.

Because of our religious backgrounds, we attended Sunday Mass together. Unlike Mark, whose religious practice had been an occasional Christmas Mass, Joe valued our shared devotion and attending services.

Sporting a jacket and dress slacks, Joe fervently bowed his head in prayer before Mass. Once the ritual began, he threw his heart into all the congregational responses, with the appropriate kneeling and sitting attitudes. His sincerity touched my heart. During the sermon, he reached over to hold my hand with a tender caress securing our spiritual bond as well. I found his large warm hand encasing my smaller cold fingers an outward expression of Joe's inner strength of character. Sitting with Joe, I found the bonds of love and the expression of love that were void in the convent. With that love came the first sprouts of joy.

At the time for us to go to the altar to receive communion, Joe rose to let me out of the pew first. I assumed he displayed his usual sense of politeness, but then he surprised me by sitting back down. I frowned wondering what could possibly be wrong that would cause Joe to decline participating in communion. As I marched up to receive the host, I worried that Joe was amiss with some deep dark secret sin. I puzzled over his declining communion, especially since worship seemed so important to him.

Later over coffee at breakfast, I inquired about his behavior. "I don't mean to pry into your personal religious practices," I tried to couch this inquisition in a friendly interested conversation. "But is there a reason that you didn't go to communion?"

"Oh, I would love to receive communion," he gushed. "But the Catholic Church has a rule against divorced people participating in communion. It says right there in the bulletin who is worthy to receive the sacrament." He lowered his eyes in embarrassment.

My blood pressure surged on Joe's behalf. Joe had gone through counseling conducted by the Diocese of Denver to save his two-year marriage. At the end, the priest told Joe that he could never make his wife happy and that he should seek an annulment. Joe's parents were so upset with the divorce that they didn't speak to him for eighteen months. Only when his final annulment papers came through from the diocese, giving the approval of the church, did his parents call him to say that they were coming for a visit. But even then, they just behaved as if nothing happened. They mentioned nothing about the lengthy lapse in communication.

I knew the betrayal Joe felt. We were kindred souls flayed by the Catholic Church. Our formative years in Catholic schools sculpted our minds. Our desire to follow the rules made us make life decisions following prescribed edicts. We both knew the pain of living our lives as others thought we should and the torment of divorce. We'd followed the rules of the church that we loved, and yet still felt the blade of its power define our relationship with God. Religious rites, rituals, and rules, rules, rules seemed to put up more roadblocks on our spiritual paths.

Leaning forward, I whispered, "Joe, you can't let your divorce get in the way of your love for God. You, of all people, need to be at the Lord's communion table. The church should not get in the way of your spirituality."

Joe and I spent many hours discussing the church and its teaching on birth control, the place of women in the Church, the presence of Hell, the belief in reincarnation, and various practices. "That's not the Catholic view," Joe argued, thinking that he had won the discussion with the weight of the church on his side. Friends had accused me of being a "cafeteria Catholic," picking what Catholic stance I would choose to believe or not believe. But I figured that there were many rooms in God's house and just as many roads to get into one of those rooms. What part of an all-loving Father didn't they understand?

My long hard fought battle within had finally broken lose with the freedom from religious bondage. I kept my belief in God and the Catholic Church, but only up against my own innate sense of spirituality. I would not let another's interpretation of religious practice dictate my personal relationship with God. The guilt beast yoked to my mind had been severed. As I railed against guilt, Joe agreed to go to the "church according to Patty."

For the third time in my life, I stood at the back of a Catholic church in preparation for marriage. Here I was, forty-five years old, as giddy as a lovesick schoolgirl, reassuring myself that once again it's never too late for happiness. I stood ready to head down the aisle for marriage number three, but this time I had made the choice without pressure from others.

"Are you ready for this, Pat?" my anxious Dad probed. The setting sun cast pinkish hues as we waited for the fifty guests to find their places to witness Joe and I exchanging wedding vows.

A few minutes earlier, I stood wearing my new white Armani suit and a white wide brim hat in front of the mirror on the wall. "Beautiful," I swooned, admiring my long brown hair falling to my shoulders, "I'm just beautiful." I almost laughed remembering the scolding I received for trying to catch my reflection in the glass on the refectory cabinets trying to see how I fared in my new novice veil. The scolding felt like ages ago in someone else's body. I celebrated this wedding marking the end of my journey rather than the beginning that I knew it really was.

Dad looked tired, but I sensed his excitement to walk me down the aisle one more time. "Joe's a wonderful man. I'm so glad that you were open to meeting him. Marrying Tom would have been a huge mistake, in my opinion," Dad reflected, looking kindly into my eyes—mirror images of his own big brown eyes. My stomach tweaked a bit with the mention of Tom's name, but I smiled remembering that this day belonged to Joe.

"I'm more than ready," I piped up feeling fortunate how things worked out for the better when Tom didn't make that trip to Idaho. The words of the psychic Edith popped into my mind. I hadn't thought of those words since the day I buried the tape recording in my bottom drawer. "You'll leave Tom in this lifetime, but you're not strong enough yet," the stout black intuitive minister predicted. I mused at her perception as the musical chords of the Canon in D echoed in the church announcing my entrance as a bride.

Butterflies fluttering in my stomach and locked in my dad's arm, I strolled down the aisle. The sweet aroma of cascading palms and orchids filled my nose, all in place for the next day's celebration of Palm Sunday. Dad kissed me good-bye at the end of the aisle, wiping his teary eyes as he handed me off to Joe who clutched my trembling hand. I fought back the welling tears at how Dad had been there for me throughout my journey.

I glanced over at mom, sitting prim clutching her ever-present, ever-pressed white linen handkerchief. She was there with me when I became Sister Mary Kateri, and she was there when I married Mark. On my parents' arms, I made it through to my last marriage.

Standing there in front of God, family, and friends, I now, for the first time, had full knowledge when speaking the marriage vows. Unlike my vows in the convent, which professed poverty, chastity, and obedience to a coercive institution, this union I freely embraced. Unlike my marriage to Mark, which was annulled on grounds of immaturity, I entered this holy matrimony in emotional adulthood. For the third time in my life at the altar of marriage, I felt the gravity of commitment. I felt like one of the beautiful white trumpet lilies, blooming with joy, and ushering in a moment of triumph.

Closing my eyes, I prayed once again, "Where are you, God? It's me again, Patty. Thank you."

"Yes, Patty, I'm here with you, like always," a voice deep within me seemed to answer. "I've been the knot in your stomach, the tears in your eyes, the red bitten lip, the lilt in your step, and the pounding of your heart. While you were busy looking for me in rites, rituals, and rules, I was here all along on the inside. I've been with you every step of the way." As God spoke, sheer contentment washed over me, and the tears that I'd held back now flowed.

Looking straight up into Joe's loving eyes, I confidently stated, "I do" with every ounce of fervor in me. Joe took his handkerchief to dab my wet cheeks trying not to smear the mascara; he knew me so well.

The ceremony ended with the organ's loud piping of *Ode to Joy*. My joy overflowed, not like the young innocent schoolgirl happy to please everyone else, but as a mature woman knowing happiness springs from the inside. Joe and I, now husband and wife, made our way back down the aisle while I reveled in the new fork in my spiritual road. My little feelings in my gut, that beckoning emotion always there, had been God all along directing me. I just hadn't listened. I had to discover myself, my freedom, and the God within.

Patty and Joe Kogutek, Wedding Day 1992

Years later after Joe and I had relocated to Montana, we attended a crowded cocktail party. Since we were new in town, a friend introduced me by dropping the "nun bomb." Exposing the nun secret usually elicited standard reactions: choking back silent gasps of horror coupled with stifling curiosity. Trying to find a way to handle the awkwardness, I engaged in my ritualistic reaction by tightening my stomach while flinging my shoulders back and smiling as if we were discussing the latest lawn furniture.

But I'd come a long way since my convent days. The habits, both woven and behavioral, changed throughout the decades. The timid obedient teen that had walked into the convent to don the black habit had blossomed into a confident well-developed woman. Instead of the black veil covering my head, long bleached blonde tresses framed my face. Instead of a heavy woolen black tunic draping to the floor, my tight red mini skirt drew attention to my long slender legs. Rather than the religious garb of the peasants, I proudly wore diamonds and a richly scented perfume, sealing the total package. My couture screamed "materialistic world." Its contrast to the nun bomb always grabbed attention.

Shaking my hand in greeting, the stately gentleman with silver streaks woven through his hair took the nun news with aplomb. Despite his casually chic attire, his blue eyes twinkled, but hinted at steel—a message that not much could be pulled over on him. He seemed to take pleasure in the nun puzzle. His eyes roamed up and down my tall stature as he pieced together the nun secret with what he saw. I squirmed on the inside.

"You couldn't have been a nun," he finally pronounced, professing his expertise with certainty as if he had just discovered a huge loophole in his biggest business deal.

"Yes, I was," I shot back, pelleting him with a certain swagger. "I was Sister Mary Kateri!" I didn't add Sister Patricia and the rest of my names.

As he assessed the picture of the worldly blonde, whose manicured hands caressed a cocktail of chilled Grey Goose, his grin widened. Smirking as he tipped his amber scotch in a toast, he proclaimed in baptismal fashion, "But you're more like Sister Mary Vodka."

The names associated with guilt and the convent had finally given way to another name—but one that I could live with. One that brought a smile to everyone's face. The nickname stuck while its humor let me fling the tightly secretive convent doors open-wide to embrace my past.

I'd come full circle. In the convent, I was proud to be a nun and serve God. But when I left, I felt embarrassed by my nun secret, not telling a soul until my sister blabbed, announcing my past at every introduction. I found safety in hanging out with Catholics who "understood." When I look back at those formative young adult years in the convent and what I missed, I shake my head at my stupidity. But God, in His way, saved me from those years for some reason. Being so naïve, I could have been dragged down so many paths; at least, I was tucked in the safety of the convent.

Now when the nun bomb is dropped, pride wells up in me knowing that I had the strength to endure the convent and change my habits. I can look my past full in the face, knowing with full maturity and freedom, that I embrace my relationship with God, armed now with the best of His material and spiritual worlds.

"You really were a nun?"

"Yes, I really was. And now? Now, I'm Sister Mary Vodka."

Epilogue

October 2011: Where Are They Now?

The Servants of Mary convent that I entered in 1965 is still in operation, but like me, it has changed over the years. Then, our convent had 266 members with an average age of forty-nine years old. Between the years of 1969-1973, concurrent with Vatican II reforms, the Servants of Mary lost thirty-seven nuns. By 2010, a mere eighty-four nuns comprised the order with the average age of seventy-five years. Only a handful of nuns were under sixty years old.

I entered the convent with nine postulants, eight of us coming fresh from high school at eighteen years old. But only one of us took final vows and still serves as a nun. Today, the order does not accept candidates directly out of high school. The girl must be mature, having life experiences, her college education, and knowing that she truly desires to be a nun. Young women are not turning to the convent as in the past. Large Catholic families have dwindled, and an increase in career opportunities allows more choices for women than the traditional 1960s professions of secretary, teacher, nurse, or nun. Today, no candidates-in-training are studying to be nuns in the Servants of Mary convent.

Running like clockwork, the once self-sufficient Motherhouse of the 1960s relied on the postulants and novices for cleaning, food preparation, and cooking. The Motherhouse now hires out cleaning and food preparation while an entire floor of the convent serves as an infirmary for aging nuns.

When I lived in the convent, all nuns worked in education, staffing Catholic elementary and high schools in seven states. Today, only twenty-nine percent of the nuns work in traditional education. In contrast to bustling nuns rushing off to staff entire schools, their charitable endeavors are now spread thin across communities where they serve as pastoral ministers, counselors, and educators. Nuns now have a choice as to their ministries. Some have found a calling to other forms of service such as healing touch, massage, and working in food banks or at St. Vincent de Paul centers. The order operates the St. Peregrine Ministry that gives support, prayers, and encouragement to those individuals and families suffering from serious illness. Requests for their services come from around the world.

In 1995, I went back to my thirtieth high school reunion and attended Mass in my same convent chapel. In that chapel, where I laid on the floor swearing to live the vows of poverty, chastity, and obedience, I carried the bread and wine in the offertory procession wearing a sleeveless dress revealing unholy arms and a mini skirt that would have failed to reach the ground when kneeling. How far the Catholic Church and I had come!

Facing my past with trepidation, I recently had the opportunity to visit the Motherhouse to meet with the Provincial, tour the newly remodeled buildings, and chat with some of my nun friends. I hadn't had much contact with them over the years, so this was a special visit. I relived many of the scenes in this book as I strolled through the halls and reconnected with devoted women with whom I once shared the convent life. We finally had the opportunity to discuss our novitiate years with each other, and many of their feelings rang with the same tunes as mine.

The convent changed in the past forty-some years to meet the needs of modern nuns serving the community. Moved walls, remodeled rooms, an updated chapel, and comfy furniture have made the convent more of a home. When touring the novitiate, I smiled at the sign that said "Men" on a restroom door-indicating just how far religious life has come.. But amidst all the change, most impressive was the heart of soul of the order: reaching out to all with constant service and compassion.

AND WHAT ABOUT ME?

After I left the convent, my devotion and service to the Catholic Church have changed from attending daily Mass to working as a Eucharistic minister, delivering Meals on Wheels, and volunteering for Hospice. I raised money for numerous local charities, including chairing a campaign that raised six million dollars to build a state of the art facility for North Valley Hospital in Whitefish, Montana. Ten percent of the net proceeds of this book will be donated to North Valley Hospital and the Servants of Mary convent in Omaha, Nebraska to help support the caring and healing that both institutions provide for those in need.

My faith has never been stronger, moving from an externally based set of religious rules to an internally motivated spirituality. This new orientation may include a few theories outside traditional Catholic thinking, but I'm comfortable with that. I'm on my joyful journey, daily seeking spiritual communion with God, guilt left aside.

But alas, I still struggle with some ingrained habits such as blindly following orders from those in authority. When flying home to Montana recently, I stood in line with five other passengers to use the lavatory. As we waited, the pilot asked everyone to sit down due to turbulence. Without hesitation, I returned to my seat. But the other four passengers remained in the aisle ignoring the captain. If I blindly follow the voice of the captain, no wonder I ran into the convent thinking I heard the voice of God!

And what about my three marriages—to God, to Mark, and to Joe? Joe has outlasted the others! Entering our third decade of marriage, we split our time between Montana and Arizona.

My prayer is that you gleaned a lesson or two from my life's path from Sister Mary Kateri to Sister Mary Vodka. If you see a car with a license plate reading "SMV," give me honk...and a prayer.

Afterword

When I first met Patty, we fast became soul mates. We commiserated about our upbringings in very strict Catholic male-dominated families and how we plodded through life trying to break out of our patterns of guilt for pleasing others. Our strong fathers who ruled the roost reinforced the expectations from God and the church that we had to be perfect. My father's famous words echoed through me for decades, "If you're not going to do it right, don't do it at all." The mindset that everything I did had to be perfect smothered me with guilt.

Patty's early struggles in and following the convent prepared her well to understand me. Even better than I understood myself. She helped me see the importance of discovering the force that ultimately dwells within. The journey we embarked on together some twenty-odd years ago has been the most joyful and liberating time of my life. As I slowly broke free of the chains of guilt and religious rituals, I discovered the confidence that accompanies the true spirituality within.

The steps that Patty discovered on her journey were an incredible help to me; I am eternally grateful for the freedom they have provided. It is an honor and a privilege to be able to share my life with someone who keeps helping me grow, and I look forward to the next two decades and more with the love of my life.

—Joe Kogutek

A Note from Patty

I hope you enjoyed taking my spiritual journey. Reviews are the best gift an author can receive. Not only do reviews give us insights on how our message is being received, but also encourage us. Please take a minute to post a review on the site where you bought the book—it's generally very easy to do. I'd be "eternally grateful."

—Patty Ptak Kogutek

Acknowledgements

In recognition of Sylvia Browne whose insightful reading planted the initial stirring of this book.

I'd like to acknowledge Becky Lomax with special benediction for her invaluable help as writing coach and editor of this book. Her overall support in prodding me to dig deeper, even to the point of tears, allowed me to unveil buried emotions and put them into beautiful words.

In appreciation to Sharon Lechter, Greg Tobin, Jennifer A. Murphy, and Suzanne Zaccone for their input, guidance, and valuable suggestions.

Thanks also to Valerie Crosby and her team at Crosby Wright for bringing the artistic design to this book.

I'm very grateful to Nick Bunick, Gerry Gavin, Sharon Lechter, Adrina Trigiani, Loree Bischoff Aaron Harper, Constance Holcomb, Walter Serwatka, and Dr. Coleene Fernando for their feedback, contribution of ideas, testimonials and constant support.

Heartfelt appreciation goes to my fellow writers, Phyllis, Dawn, and Sue from the Flathead Authors Group and the Scottsdale Society of Women Writers for their willingness to embrace the novice.

All my love goes to my husband Joe who had more faith in my capabilities to write a book than I did.

And to my readers, thank you, for your inspiration and reason to share the journey.

Book Club Discussion Questions

1. You don't have to go into the convent to lose your happiness, what kind of thinking contributed to Patty's loss of happiness. What can people do to protect their own happiness?

2. Patty was raised in the trifecta of religious environments, church, school, and family. What could the family have done to protect their daughter's immature decision?

3. Raising children to be morally responsible is a tough task. How do you instill values in your children without creating a "guilt sponge" – based on fear?

4. Patty's mom feels guilty about her part in Patty's unhappiness. What would you tell her mother?

5. What is the main difference between religion and spirituality? Can you think of situations in a child's life that might stifle spirituality?

About the Author

After receiving her doctorate from the University of Southern California and her marriage to Joe, the couple moved to Whitefish, MT now splitting their time between Montana and Phoenix, AZ. Patty never imagined that "retirement" could be so demanding after working as an elementary school Principal and coordinator at the San Diego Office County Office of Education. Patty works with The Scotttsdale Society of Women Writers in AZ and the Authors of the Flathead in MT. She continues her love of teaching with workshops, speaking engagements and volunteering with her favorite charities. She also serves on the Board of North Valley Hospital Foundations Board in Whitefish, MT.

Want to find God in your everyday life? Watch for the upcoming release of "G-vites: Everyday Invitations From God".

To be put on mailing list for advanced copies and special inner circle giveaways, go to PattyKogutek.com and let me know where to send it.

Contact Information

Let's stay in touch. Here's my contact information:

Website: http://pattykogutek.com

Weekly Blog: http://pattykogutek.com/spiritually-speaking/

Daily Inspiration: http://pattykogutek.com/inspirational-insights/

Twitter: https://twitter.com/pattykogutek

Facebook: https://www.facebook.com/Patty-Kogutek-Author-263832907009510/timeline/

Pinterest: https://www.pinterest.com/pkogutek/

Instagram: https://instagram.com/pattykogutek_inspiration/

Appendix

7 Secrets to Guilt-free Living

Secret One
Don't let religion get in the way of your relationship with God.

Secret Two
Life is not a matter of chance, but of choices we make along the way.

Secret Three
"You can't steal second base until you take your foot off first."
—Frederick B. Wilcox

Secret Four
Don't worry about making a good decision;
instead make a decision good.

Secret Five
"Good judgment comes from experience.
Experience comes from bad judgment."
—Chinese Fortune Cookie

Secret Six
"When the student is ready, the teacher will appear."
—Zen Proverb

Secret Seven
Happiness is not a gift, but a skill.

Glossary

Chapter of Faults A weekly assembly of nuns who engage in self-assessment to acknowledge faults and receive corrections for infractions of religious rules.

Compline The night prayer of the Divine Office. This is the final office prayer before retiring, signaling the completion of the day.

Convent A religious community founded to perform a mission of charitable works following certain rules under the direction of a superior.

Divine Office Sometimes referred to as the Liturgy of the Hours reflecting "round the clock prayer." Designated psalms or canticles are to be sung or recited at specific times of the day, which are Matins, Lauds, Vespers, and Compline.

Habit A unique set of garments worn by religious orders signifying a lifestyle of dedication. Traditional habits include a tunic, scapular, wimple, and veil.

Junior Professed Nun Nuns who have taken temporary vows valid for two or three years before their final profession of vows for life.

Lauds The morning prayer of the Divine Office, sometimes prayed later in the morning following Matins.

Liturgical Hours Another name for Divine Office.

Matins	Traditionally the Hour of Matins was to be prayed at midnight. For convenience, this together with Lauds greeted the day.
Motherhouse	The home base and center of operation for a religious community of nuns.
Mother Provincial	The head superior in charge of the religious province, which could include a large geographical region of several states.
Novices	The second year candidates in the novitiate. Novices wear the entire black habit, but with a while veil.
Novitiate	The place where candidates to be nuns live, and the two-year training period for religious candidates to prepare for temporary vows includes first year postulants and second year novices.
Order	An organization of nuns in a religious community set apart by certain rules of religious practices based on the founder's devotion and mission of charity.
Plainsong	Liturgical music chanted or sung without accompaniment. Sometime called plainchant or Gregorian chant.
Postulants	First year candidates to be nuns in the novitiate.
Professed Nuns	Those nuns who have progressed through the years of training to take final vows for life. Training included one year as a postulant, one year as a novice, and five years as a junior professed nun.
Refectory	Dining room.
Rosary	A prescribed pattern of prayers consisting of the recitation Hail Marys and Our Fathers. Moving one's fingers along rosary beads keeps track of the number of prayers recited.

Sacristan	A designated nun in charge of setting up the chapel for Mass.
Scapular	An article of the traditional religious habit consisting of two pieces of wool cloth connected at the shoulder and worn over the tunic like an apron. It symbolized the yoke of Christ and a sign of protection.
Tunic	The loose-fitting, black serge, primary part of the traditional habit. It resembles the Latin toga, but draped to floor length for nuns and hung with long sleeves.
Vatican II	This second Vatican Council convened from 1962-1965 to address the relationship between the Catholic Church and the modern world. Vatican II, which called for the Church's renewal and reform, abandoned the Latin liturgy and many century-old rituals.
Veil	A black or white article of the traditional habit worn over the head. It symbolized purity and virginity for nuns as Brides of Christ.
Vespers	The evening prayer of the Divine Office. Often prayed before the evening meal.
Vocation	A special grace, calling, and gift given by God to a select few to serve Him in a consecrated life as a religious nun or priest.
Wimple	A part of the traditional habit consisting of white starched cloth worn around the neck, resembling a short bib. The wimple evolved from medieval times when it was worn as a headscarf around the neck as a sign of submission.